# CONTENTS

# INTRODUCTION

The outdoors is a BIG place and there are endless adventures and fun activities waiting for you outside. This book gives you all sorts of ideas for fun things you can do in the garden, at the beach, in the countryside, and in town. There are summer activities, winter ideas, things you can make outdoors, instructions to build wacky dens and loads of brilliant games to play. The book also has 37 special outdoor challenges at the end, which are bigger and tougher family activities for you to try. So, turn off the TV, put on your shoes, open the door and prepare to have an amazing time!

## STAY SAFE!

There's a huge amount of fun to be had outdoors, but you do need to remember these important things:
- Make sure there's an adult with you when you're out and about
- Take extra care near water
- Watch and listen for traffic when you're near roads
- Avoid too much sun: use sun cream and wear a hat

ANTI-BOREDOM

# Community Learning & Libraries
## *Cymuned Ddysgu a Llyfrgelloedd*

This item should be returned or renewed by the last date stamped below.

*CIN*

Newport
CITY COUNCIL
CYNGOR DINAS
Casnewydd

To renew visit:

**www.newport.gov.uk/libraries**

# To the children and staff of Churchfield Primary School

Bloomsbury Children's Books
An imprint of Bloomsbury Publishing Plc

50 Bedford Square
London
WC1B 3DP
UK

www.bloomsbury.com

First published in 2017 by Bloomsbury Children's Books

Copyright © Andy Seed, 2017
Illustrations copyright © Scott Garrett, 2017

British Library Cataloguing-in-Publication Data
A catalogue record for this book is available from the British Library.

ISBN
PB: 978-1-4088-7009-9

2 4 6 8 10 9 7 5 3 1

Printed and bound in the UK by CPI Group (UK) Ltd, Croydon CR0 4YY

MIX
Paper from
responsible sources
FSC® C020471

To find out more about our authors and books visit www.bloomsbury.com. Here you will find extracts, author interviews, details of forthcoming events and the option to sign up for our newsletters.

All activities away from the garden should be supervised by an adult and appropriate precautions should be taken to make sure that everyone stays safe. Particular care should be taken near water. In summer it's advisable for children to wear a hat and use sun cream.

## IMPORTANT:
The author and publisher recommend enabling SafeSearch when using the internet in conjunction with this book. We can accept no responsibility for information published on the internet.

# GARDEN FUN

Gardens can be boring — but not now you have this book! In this section you'll find LOADS of fun things to do in a garden. Most of them use everyday things, some of them are easy, some of them take a bit longer but all of them will be brilliant to try. Just remember not to destroy the garden in the process!

# Love, hate or meh?

What's your verdict on these things found in gardens? Give them a score out of ten.

Fire pit

BBQ

Swing

Pond

Giant chess

Gnomes

Slide

Orchard

Summer house

Stream

Basketball stand

# Make a den

Garden dens are loads of fun. You can eat in them, play games in them, read in them, shelter from the sun if it's hot, or just mess about with your friends. Here are three different garden dens you can have a go at building.

## 1. Tipi den
### Get started

**1** Tie the canes together with the string or wire about 20cm from one end, wrapping the string around them several times.

**2** Stand the canes up and spread them out to make a classic wigwam or tipi shape.

**3** Peg the sheets to the canes so that the wigwam is covered. Add a blanket inside and you're done!

# 2. String and sheet den
## Get started

**1** Tie the string between two trees about 1.5 metres up. Wrap the string around the tree trunks several times so that it doesn't slip down.

## Stuff you need

- Some strong string
- An old blanket
- 3 or 4 large sheets
- Some clothes pegs
- Tent pegs (or heavy items such as stones or pieces of wood)

**2** Drape the long edge of one sheet to the string and peg it well.

**3** Push a line of tent pegs into the ground about 1m to the side of the string and peg the other edge of the sheet to these. You can also put heavy items like stones on the sheet to hold it down.

**4** Repeat this on the other side with another sheet.

**5** Peg a third sheet to cover one end, add a blanket inside and you have a great den!

# 3. Fence and chair den

## Get started

- **3 or 4 sturdy chairs**
- Some large books or other heavy items
- **An old blanket**
- 3 or 4 large sheets
- **Some clothes pegs**

**1** Drape one edge of a big sheet over a fence and use pegs to fix it to the fence.

**2** Drape the other end of the sheet over the chairs.

**3** Put the heavy books on the chairs to stop them tipping.

**4** Peg the sheet to the chairs, peg another sheet to one open end of the den, add a blanket inside and it's ready.

# Create a bird hide

Birds are beautiful and amazing creatures, and one of the best ways to get close to them in the garden is to build a simple bird hide. You can hide in this and spy on the birds visiting a bird table or food put out for them on the ground.

## Stuff you need

- 3 long sticks (over 1.5m long)
- String
- Lots of small cuttings or branches from trees or bushes (ask a parent for the best place to get these and the sticks)
- A stool

## Get started

**1** Make a simple frame from the sticks, tying them with the string like this:

**2** Wrap string around the sticks leaving one side open:

**3** Hang the cuttings and leafy branches over the string so the hide is hidden and well camouflaged.

**4** Hide inside very quietly on your stool and make a note of the birds you see.

# Set up a bug trap

## Stuff you need

- A large plastic tub with steep sides, e.g. ice-cream container
- A trowel
- 4 small stones
- A flat piece of wood or tile

Gardens are full of creepy-crawlies, minibeasts, strange insects and bugs — and here is a good way to catch some so you can study them. It will help to have a guide book of some sort so you can identify what you have caught.

## Get started

**1** Find a corner of the garden which is shady and flat.

**2** Dig a hole just a bit larger than the plastic container.

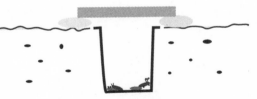

**3** Put the container in the hole then fill in the soil around it so there are no gaps — the edge must be level with the soil.

**4** Put the stones around it and lay the wood or tile on them to shade the container.

**5** To attract more bugs place some bits of fruit such as banana in the trap.

**6** Handle your minibeasts with care and remember to return them to the wild when you have finished looking at them.

# ❀ Treasure hunt

Treasure hunts are loads of fun and there are lots of ways to do them. Here's a simple one to try with a group. You could ask an adult to do the clues or do them yourself for friends or family to find. It's easy in a big garden but if you don't have much space you just need to be creative! You can put some clues indoors as well.

## Stuff you need

- Some treasure (edible treasure is good such as a bag of sweets – make sure it's waterproof)
- Two pieces of plain or lined paper
- Scissors
- A pen

## Get started

**1** On a piece of paper write the heading 'Answers' and put the numbers 1-6 down the left hand side.

**2** Go around the garden spotting good places to hide clues and, most important of all, somewhere to hide the treasure.

**3** Hide the treasure first – it should be under an object or inside something or behind something. Write down where you have hidden it next to number 6 on the paper.

**4** Write down five other places where you are going to hide clues. Again they should be near, in or under something that you can write down. Put these five on the list.

**5** To make the clues cut another piece of paper in half then cut each half into three so you have six clues. Number these 1 to 6.

**6** Write clue 1: this will lead to hiding place number 1. If hiding place 1 is, for example, behind the shed, the clue might say, "Look by a place which rhymes with bed" or "Rearrange HEDS to find this place". Do not hide clue 1 – this will be given to the searchers. The thing hidden in place 1 will be clue 2!

**7** Do this for the other clues: each clue leads to the next clue and clue 6 leads to the treasure. Here are some other examples of hiding places and clues:

❀ **Greenhouse** ("hot home of tomatoes" or "You'll find this under glass")

❀ **Bird table** ("Where sparrows feast" or "this table has no chairs but who cares?")

❀ **Hanging basket** ("swinging home of the highest flowers" or "No shopping in this basket")

❀ **Garden bench** ("somewhere for a rest?" or "rearrange teas" [seat])

❀ **Compost heap** ("burial place of dead grass" or "hot pongy pile").

**8** When it's all ready hand over clue 1 to the searchers and watch them scurry about!

# Grow herbs

Herbs are excellent to grow because they do well in containers and they're quite easy to get started. You don't even need a garden – just a small space outside. Herbs also smell wonderful and you can eat them!

## Stuff you need

- Some herb seeds: good ones to try are chives, parsley, mint and basil
- Some containers: plant pots or tubs are best, or you can use old yoghurt pots or ice-cream cartons
- Compost or soil
- A watering can
- Labels – lolly sticks are good

## Get started

1 Fill your containers with compost or soil nearly to the top (this can get messy so do it outside).

2 Water the compost well with the watering can.

3 Open the seed packet carefully and tip some seeds onto a piece of paper. With your fingers sprinkle a few seeds over the wet compost, spreading them out as best you can.

4 Take a handful of compost from the bag (make sure it has no lumps) and sprinkle it over the seeds – you must aim to just cover them, not bury them deep!

5 Add a label for each pot so you know what is in it.

6 You need to make sure that the compost doesn't dry out. A good way to do this is to cover the pot with a clear plastic bag (tucked underneath so it can't blow off if it's outside).

7 Check your seeds after a few days. They should start to grow in about a week. Herbs like a sunny spot outdoors – remember to keep watering them!

# Water balloon piñata

A piñata is a hollow hanging object that you hit with a stick to break it open. They usually have sweets inside but these ones have water! This is brilliant for a baking hot day.

## Stuff you need

- Water balloons (water bombs) – you can get these from party shops or online
- Strong string – thin cotton won't do!
- Clothes pegs
- A long cardboard tube (like you get inside wrapping paper). You can also make a stick by tightly rolling newspaper and taping it

## Get started

1 Hanging the balloons up is the tricky bit – you may need adult help with this.

2 Tie a long piece of string between two trees or strong posts or walls. It will need to be at least 2m above the ground and as tight as possible. (Or you can use a washing line.)

3 Fill 5 or 6 water balloons with water and tie them.

4 Peg the balloons to the horizontal string, well spread out, so that they hang down.

5 Take turns to whack the balloons with the tube or stick – one each! You can play the game blindfolded for even more fun!

# Sunflower competition

Sunflowers are brilliant because they can grow so huge: 4 metres tall if you are lucky. You don't even need a garden – a balcony or small outside space will do. This is an activity for a group to try – the idea is to grow the tallest sunflower, of course!

## Get started

1. The best time to sow your sunflower seeds is late spring – the packet will tell you which month is best.

2. Read the seed packet instructions for the best way to sow them. Sow them straight into the ground (in a sunny, sheltered spot).

3. Make sure that you water the seeds in the soil or compost.

4. Put labels in the ground so you know whose sunflower is whose. Keep weeds away. While the plants are small, you can keep slugs and snails off with half a clear plastic bottle placed over the plants.

## Stuff you need

- A packet of sunflower seeds (make sure it's a tall variety)
- Some plant pots and compost
- **Some plant labels and a pen (lolly sticks will do)**
- Strong canes and garden string

5. When the sunflowers are about 10-20cm high, stick canes in the soil to support the plants, using loose twists of string to tie the plants to the canes.

6. By mid summer they should be getting really big and flowering. Use a tape measure to discover the champion!

# Soap slide

A home-made soap slide in your garden is truly a wonderful thing. You will need a reasonably big lawn, at least 10m long, or you'll need to go to the park. A hot sunny day is the best time to do this – get your swimming costumes on!

## Stuff you need

• A large plastic drinks bottle
• A piece of polythene sheet 2m wide and at least 6m long (the longer the better) – you can buy this from garden centres and DIY stores
• Washing up liquid
• A hosepipe (optional)

## Get started

1. If your lawn is on a slope, that's perfect, but you can still make a slide on level ground.
2. Lay the polythene on the ground, allowing a few metres for a run-up. Make sure there's nothing to crash into at the end!
3. Squirt washing-up liquid into the plastic bottle until it's about 4cm deep. Add warm water until the bottle is full. Tip the bottle to mix it well.

4. Pour some of the soapy mixture over the polythene sheet so there's a good covering all the way along – don't use it all! Spread it out well.
5. Have a test slide – remember to wear a swimming costume as you'll get very wet and soapy! You may need to fix down the front of the sheet – this can be done by laying a mat over the front edge. Now you're ready to play!
6. Add more soap mixture as needed. You can also keep the slide wet with the hose set to light spray.

17

# Make a rainbow

Who doesn't love a rainbow? But did you know that you can make your own garden rainbow? You just need a hose and a sunny day! Warning: you're probably going to get wet, so wear a swimming costume or waterproofs!

## Stuff you need

- A garden hose (connected to a tap!)
- A spray attachment or sprinkler

## Get started

**1** This does only work on a sunny day so there's no point trying it if the weather is cloudy!

**2** Ask an adult to connect up the hose with the sprinkler or spray set to a fine spray.

**3** Stand with your back to the sun and switch on the spray – you should see a fantastic rainbow arc in the spray (you might even get a full circle if you aim upwards).

**4** If you don't have a sprinkler or spray you can try putting your thumb over the end of the hosepipe to make it spray.

# Make a tunnel

Crawling through real tunnels is not advisable but you can easily make a safe, fun tunnel in your garden using the plans below.

## Get started

**1** Make hoops for the tunnel by pushing the cane pieces into the ground halfway then attaching the hosepipe sections to them:

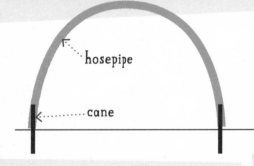

hosepipe

cane

**2** Make a series of these hoops then drape sheets and blankets over them.

**3** You'll need to hold down the edges of the sheets with heavy objects. Shoes are quite useful for this! Or you can peg the blanket to the hoops.

## Stuff you need

- Several large blankets or sheets (make sure you ask which ones you can use)
- Netting (optional)
- Some pieces of old hosepipe cut into 1m lengths (ask an adult to do this)
- Some garden canes cut into 30cm pieces (ask an adult to do this)
- Large cardboard boxes with lid flaps (optional)
- Clothes pegs

**4** You can also add boxes to the tunnel. Open out all of the flaps except one of the small ones. Tape this to the sides of the box to stop it collapsing.

**5** You can also drape netting over the hoops and add leafy branches and twigs to this.

19

# Experiment with potions

Being a wacky scientist for a day can be a lot of fun if you do it outside where you can make more mess. Just make sure you wear old clothes and don't create any evil monsters that will disturb the neighbours.

## Stuff you need

- An outdoor table or flat surface to work on, covered with a plastic cloth
- Different sized plastic bottles and containers
- Jugs, a funnel, spoons
- Water, food colouring, vinegar, bicarbonate of soda, cornflour, washing up liquid

## Get started

1. This is very messy so make sure you're well away from anything that doesn't like mess!
2. When you are ready, try mixing up some of the ingredients and see what happens. Beware: adding vinegar to bicarbonate of soda makes a LOT of fizz!
3. Colour your potions with food colouring for extra zing in your lab.
4. If you can, put samples of the potions into small bottles or jars with lids and label them, letting your

imagination go potty: Burp Juice, Frog Snot, Villain Vanishing Tonic, Blood of Moody Aliens...
5. Don't drink any of the potions – you'll probably be sick!

# Camp overnight

If you've never camped the night in your garden before then you are in for a treat. Make sure you ask first or your parents might get a shock at seeing a tent by the house at midnight!

## Stuff you need

★ **A tent (ask to borrow one if you don't have one)**
★ Foam mats or inflatable mattresses to sleep on (optional)
★ **Sleeping bags, blankets and pillows**
★ Torches and creepy stories (optional!)
★ **Snacks and drinks**

## Get started

**1** Put up your tent and make it comfortable inside.

**2** You can have supper outside for fun too. Or save your snacks for a midnight feast!

**3** As it gets dark tell each other spooky tales, or read some creepy stories by torchlight. You can add battery-powered fairy lights too.

**4** When it's late peep outside to look for interesting things in the dark: stars in the night sky, passing satellites, foxes, owls and mice, bats or naughty cats for example.

**5** Try and get some sleep – this might not be easy if you are having too much fun!

# Plan a picnic

If the weather is good then what is more enjoyable than eating outdoors? You can plan a picnic to have in the garden – the beauty of this is that it's much easier to carry everything you need.

## Stuff you need

- **A picnic blanket or large sheet (if the grass is damp then put a waterproof tarpaulin or plastic sheet under it)**
- Paper and pens to plan the picnic
- **Plates, cups, knives, forks and food containers. Plastic cutlery and plastic or paper plates and cups are good for picnics**
- Drinks – jugs are good because they don't tip over as easily as bottles
- Food – it's always best if you make it yourself!
- **Trays to carry things (banana boxes are good for this too)**

# Get started

**1** First of all check what you're allowed to eat and drink!

**2** Start planning your picnic by writing down ideas.

**3** It's a good idea to plan something savoury, something sweet and some drinks.

**4** Here are some ideas to make and to buy:

| PICNIC IDEAS | TO MAKE | TO BUY |
|---|---|---|
| SAVOURY | Sandwiches/wraps<br>Mini-pizzas<br>Coleslaw<br>Carrot sticks | Sausage rolls<br>Samosas<br>Cherry tomatoes<br>Crisps |
| SWEET | Flapjack<br>Cupcakes<br>Cookies<br>Fruit salad | **Strawberries**<br>**Blueberries**<br>**Cake**<br>**Ice cream** |
| DRINKS | **Lemonade**<br>**Fruit juice cocktails** | Exotic juice<br>Sparkling water |

# Grow some food

There's nothing tastier than your own home-grown grub, so why not have a go at growing some delicious salads and vegetables. You don't even need a garden, just some space outside for containers. The best time to start is spring.

## Stuff you need

- **Seeds: the easiest things to try are lettuce, radishes and potatoes**
- Plants: strawberries and tomatoes can be bought as small pot plants
- **Pots or containers: the bigger the better**
- Compost or soil to fill the containers
- **Watering can**

## Get started

1. The small plants can either be planted in the soil if you have space or in containers. Either way, a sunny sheltered spot is best.

2. When sowing the seeds, follow the instructions on the packet carefully. Keep the soil moist or the seeds won't germinate (sprout).

3. If you start seeds in pots you can cover these with plastic bags until they sprout (to keep them moist).

4. If you buy small plants make sure you water them well when you put them into the ground or in larger containers. Water all the plants well in dry weather.

5. With lettuce you can just pull off leaves and the plant will keep growing. New potatoes will be ready to dig up when the plants start to flower.

# Grow some flowers

Gardening is a lot more fun than most kids realise and if you can grow some colourful flowers in the garden you'll be popular with everyone.

## Stuff you need

- Seeds: some easy flowers to try are nasturtiums, marigolds and sweet peas
- Plants: you can also buy small plants from garden centres then plant them out (move them into a bigger pot or container or into the ground)
- Pots or containers: the bigger the better
- Compost or soil to fill the containers
- Watering can

## Get started

This is the same as for vegetables:

1. Plant your seeds or small plants either straight into the ground if you have space or in containers. A sunny sheltered spot is best either way.

2. When sowing the seeds, follow the instructions on the packet carefully. Keep the soil moist or the seeds won't germinate.

3. If you start seeds in pots you can cover the pots with plastic bags until the seeds sprout (to keep them moist).

4. If you buy small plants make sure you water them well when you put them into the ground or in larger containers. Water all the plants well in dry weather.

25

# Do the close-up photo challenge

This is something really different that you can try. You may need help from an adult to set up the camera but after that it's easy!

## Stuff you need

- A digital camera – you need one that can take good close-up pictures
- A laptop or tablet to show the pictures on
- Some pencils and paper

## Get started

1. This is all about taking extreme close-up photos of things outside, then getting people to guess what they are.

2. The first thing to do is to practise taking close up photos: you need to be really close to the thing you are photographing or the pictures will be too easy to guess! This is where you may need help to set up the camera in the best mode ('macro' is good if you have it).

3. Try and take pictures from unusual angles or zoom in on a less familiar part of an object, e.g. the underside of a wheelbarrow, tree bark, moss, a shed lock, the spring of a trampoline, the pedal of a bike, an unusual leaf.

4. Look at the photos on a laptop or tablet and make sure they are in focus and not too easy to guess.

5. Decide on your best photos, show them on screen where everyone can see, then get people to write them down before revealing the answers.

# Guess

Ask a group of people to guess these – nearest wins.

1. Bamboo is the fastest-growing plant in the world. How many centimetres can the fastest type grow in one day? [91cm]

2. Kew Gardens in London lists all known plant names. How many different names does the bluebell have? [26]

3. How many people can fit into one of the world's largest treehouses at Alnwick Gardens, Northumberland, UK? [300]

4. How many bulbs are planted in the Keukenhof Gardens in Holland each year? [7 million]

# Fun Facts

Here are some things you probably never knew about tomatoes:

Heinz® Tomato Ketchup has a speed limit. It is rejected from the factory if it pours at more than 0.045 kilometres (0.028mph) an hour!

There is a festival in Spain each year where people throw 150,000 squishy tomatoes at each other.

There are over 7000 types of tomato.

Not all tomatoes are red: they can be yellow, purple, white and even black.

As they ripen, tomatoes give off small amounts of an explosive gas called ethylene.

# Snail races

You can have lots of giggles finding snails and discovering whose is the speed king!

## Stuff you need

- Garden snails (they like to hide in damp places, for example under bits of wood, among old plant pots and among large leaves in shady parts of the garden)
- An old large plate
- Coloured stickers

## Get started

**1** Each person chooses a snail and adds their own coloured sticker to its shell.

**2** Put the plate on some grass outside.

**3** Place the snails in the middle of the plate. Be gentle with them!

**4** The winner is the first one whose snail reaches the edge.

# Talk

Here are some good things to chat about:

☞ **Have you ever grown anything? What happened?**

☞ **What three special things would you have in your ideal garden?**

☞ **What's the best garden you've ever been to?**

# Choose

Imagine you could only pick one from each pair to go in your garden:

🌷 **Trampoline or swing boat?**

🌷 **Maze or log cabin?**

🌷 **Swimming pool or tree house?**

🌷 **Zip wire or tennis court?**

🌷 **Rope swing or football goal?**

🌷 **Tipi or half-pipe?**

# Garden jokes

What's red and invisible?
No tomatoes

Which flower does everyone have on their face?
Tulips

Mum: Sally, will you help me dig up some potatoes?
Sally: Why did you bury them in the first place?

What do you get if you sow light bulbs?
A power plant

Gardener: I always put manure on my rhubarb
Kid: I prefer custard

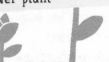

Ed: Why are you doing the splits in the garden?
Fred: This seed packet says 'plant two feet apart'

## Veg Quest

Which vegetable is the....

Fastest?          Runner beans
Wettest?          Leeks
Coldest?          Chilli peppers
Widest?           Broad beans
Most dangerous at sea?  Iceberg lettuce
Smelliest?        Pea

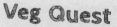

# THINGS TO MAKE

If you like making stuff you'll love this section — and there are plenty of easy mini-projects even if you're not so keen. Remember that this book is all about getting outdoors so try doing your making outside if the weather is OK.

# Parachute

Not everyone will get the chance to do a real parachute jump but anyone can make this mini one and see how they work. This is a bit fiddly but worth the trouble.

## Get started

1. First you need to cut out a square of plastic from the bin bag — it should be around 30cm each side.

2. Cut four lengths of string 40cm long.

3. Twist one of the corners of the plastic square quite tightly and place this on a table so that the twisted edge sticks out over the edge — put the cup on this to stop it unravelling.

## Stuff you need

- **A polythene bin bag**
- Thin string
- **Blu-tack or plasticine**
- Scissors, a paperclip and a heavy cup

4. Tie one piece of string tightly to the twisted corner. Do this for all four corners.

5. Tie the other ends of the four strings together. Open out the paperclip, hook this onto the string and add a blob of blu tack or plasticine to the hook.

6. Hold the parachute in the middle and drop it to see how it falls. Try rolling it up carefully, throw it upwards outside and see how it drops. Adjust the weight to make it fall slowly.

# Snapper

What's not to love about a piece of paper that makes a bang? Here's a simple way to make a noisy paper snapper.

## Get started

**1** First, fold a third of the paper over and crease it so it looks like this:

**2** Fold the right-hand third over like this....

**3** Then fold this in half:

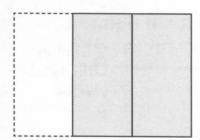

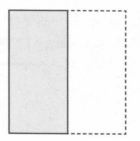

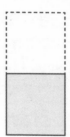

**4** Here's the tricky bit: find the two corners of the paper inside the fold and pull these down so that they stick out a little then hold the folded corners below this:

**5** It's ready to pop! Snap the snapper down sharply with your arm so it makes a bang.

# Paper spinner

## Stuff you need

- A piece of A4 paper
- Paperclips
- Scissors, a ruler and pencil

This low-tech helicopter is very easy to make. You can have competitions with your friends to see whose will stay in the air longest.

## Get started

**1** First, fold the paper in half one way and then the other. Open out and cut along the lines to make four quarters.

**2** Place a ruler against the top edge of one of the small pieces and draw a line across. Then put the ruler against the long edges to draw two more lines as shown:

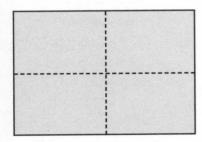

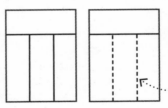

**3** Cut where the dotted lines are.

**4** Fold the left-side flap up as shown, then turn over and do the same with the other flap.

**5** Pick up the top of the T shape and add a paperclip as shown. Hold it at the top then drop it – the spinner should spin! Try changing the design in different ways then drop it from as high as possible.

# Paper planes

## Stuff you need

- **Several sheets of A4 paper**
- **Paperclips**

There are hundreds of ways to make paper planes but they are always fun when they fly well.

## Get started

**1** Try this basic design first:

a) Fold the paper in half along its length then open out.

b) Fold the top corners into the centre, pressing hard along the crease.

c) Fold the new corners into the centre as shown.

d) Fold over the tip.

e) Fold the plane along the centre line.

f) Create the wings by folding over each flap as shown.

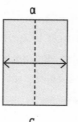

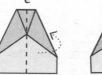
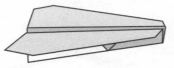

**2** Next try some adaptations:
- Fold down the edges of the wings.
- Try some small flaps at the back.
- Use a paperclip to stop the plane unfolding (or for adding weight).

**3** Look online for lots of videos and ideas for more paper plane designs. Decorate your plane and have a competition outside with prizes for distance and time in the air.

# Paper plate Frisbee

This Frisbee is cheap, easy to make and flies well. It's not so good on rainy days, though...

## Get started

**1** Put the small saucer in the centre of one of the paper plates and draw around it. Cut out the circle in the middle with the scissors. Then do the same with the other paper plate.

**2** Decorate the bottom of each paper plate ring with the felt-tip pens.

## Stuff you need

- Two paper plates
- A small saucer
- Felt-tip pens
- Scissors and a stapler

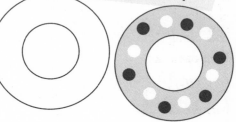

**3** Put the two paper plate rings together top to top. Staple the edges of them in 5 or 6 places.

**4** Your paper plate Frisbee is now ready to fly. You can throw it to a friend or have a competition to see who can land it nearest a target. You can even play hoopla with an upturned chair!

# Volcano

Here is an easy way to make your very own amazing erupting volcano. This is very messy so it's best to do it outside on a plastic sheet or old newspapers!

## Stuff you need

- Small plastic drinks bottle
- Dessert spoon and teaspoon
- Metal baking tray
- Sand
- Red and yellow food colouring
- Washing up liquid
- Bicarbonate of soda
- Vinegar
- A plastic jug and a funnel

## Get started

**1** Put 3 dessert spoonfuls of soda in the bottle and half fill it with warm water. Stir it well.

**2** Put the bottle on the tray and pile damp sand around it so it looks like a mini-volcano:

**3** Into the jug put 150ml of vinegar, a squirt of washing up liquid and a teaspoon of each food colouring. Stir this well.

**4** Use the funnel to quickly pour the vinegar mix into the bottle. Take the funnel out straight away and stand back: it's about to erupt!

# Giant bubble wand

You can create huge bubbles quite easily with this simple home-made wand. It works best if you leave the bubble mixture for a few days.

## Stuff you need

- **A wire coat hanger**
- A large waterproof tray or washing up bowl
- **Washing up liquid**
- Glycerine (you can find this in the baking section of the supermarket)
- **A jug and a cup**
- Tablespoon

## Get started

**1** Make the bubble mixture first: in the jug, mix a cup of washing up liquid with a cup of water. Add a tablespoon of glycerine.

**2** Make the bubble wand by pulling the wire coat hanger into an oval shape, with the handle bent upwards slightly:

**3** Take the tray outside and place it on a level surface. Carefully pour in the bubble mixture.

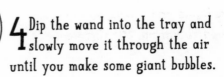

**4** Dip the wand into the tray and slowly move it through the air until you make some giant bubbles.

# Make some gloop

This can be really messy so it's best to do it outside and wear old clothes. The good thing is that it's amazing fun!

## Get started

**1** Find a good place to work outside where you can be messy. Spread out the plastic sheet or newspaper.

**2** Empty half of the cornflour into the tray then add a small amount of water. Mix this in, adding water until you have something like thick custard (but don't eat it – yuck!).

**3** Keep adding water and cornflour until it's all mixed then add a few drops of food colouring (avoiding blue or you'll get stained hands). You can also mix in some glitter for fun too.

**4** Play with the gloop seeing what it'll do – you'll find it's amazing stuff

## Stuff you need

- **A plastic basin or metal tray with sides (such as a roasting tray)**
- A packet of cornflour
- **A cup of water and a spoon**
- Food colouring
- **A plastic sheet or old newspapers**

because sometimes it acts like a liquid and sometimes it seems to be a solid. Try these experiments:
- Roll a ball of it in your hands then relax your hand.
- Hit the gloop in the tray with the palm of your hand.
- Drop a ball of gloop onto a hard surface.
- Try making a tower with it.
- Add a some shaving cream to a batch of gloop and see what happens.

**5** When you've finished, don't wash the gloop down the sink – put it in a bag in the bin.

# Woodlice maze

This is an interesting little project where you find out if a woodlouse can find its way through a maze to some food.

## Stuff you need

- Lego® bricks and a base
- A small piece of fruit or a damp leaf
- A few woodlice

## Get started

1 Build your maze first using the Lego® bricks on the base. Keep it just one brick high and quite simple. It should have a start and a finish – with fruit (or a damp leaf) at the finish line.

2 You can find woodlice in damp places in the garden: under wood or damp leaves.

3 Slip a piece of paper under the woodlice to capture them. Try to avoid touching them, but if you do touch them, be very gentle with them.

4 Place the woodlice in the maze and see if they can find their way to the finish line.

5 Make sure you put them back where you found them after they have tried the maze!

# Choose

Select your fav hobby from each pair:

**Cooking** or **sewing?**
**Electronics** or **jewellery making?**
**Lego®** building or **magic tricks?**
**Pottery** or **model aircraft?**
**Origami** or **sketching?**
**Woodworking** or **painting?**
**Gardening** or **ghost hunting?**

# Fun list

Can you make up some more of these?

| GOOD THINGS TO COLLECT | BAD THINGS TO COLLECT |
| --- | --- |
| autographs | autopilots |
| books | rooks |
| animal films | clingfilms |
| stamps | tramps |
| mugs | slugs |
| teddy bears | grizzly bears |

# Mini-book

Here's a brilliant and simple way to make a dinky little eight-page book that you can write or draw in. It's good for a rainy day or to keep a record of interesting things you have spotted.

## Get started

**1** Start with the paper in portrait format (short edge at the top). Fold in half top to bottom. Fold it in half again this way.

**2** Fold in half the other way from left to right.

**3** Open out the last two folds so that the paper is only folded in half with the crease at the bottom.

**4** Cut up from the centre line of the crease to the next crease (half way up).

**5** Hold the paper either side of the crease and bend these two rectangles away from each other.

**6** Push the pages together flat and you have a mini-book!

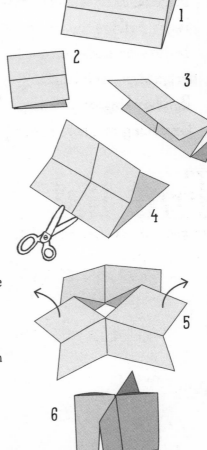

# Daisy chains

Summer is the time to make daisy chains and it's fun seeing who can make the longest one.

- Lots of daisies

## Get started

1. Pick some daisies, keeping as long a stem as possible on each.
2. Use your thumbnail to split the stem of a daisy halfway down.
3. When you've made an opening, thread another daisy through.
4. Repeat this with the new daisy, joining another to it and so on.

## Stuff you need

- Long grass

# Grass hooter

Did you know that you can make a really loud noise with just a blade of grass? Here's how.

## Get started

1. It's important to pick the right kind of grass to make this work. It needs to be a flat leaf (not a thin stem), wide and long.
2. The tricky bit is to hold the grass correctly between the base and top of your thumbs as shown.
3. Try to stretch the grass tightly then blow through the small gap between your thumbs where the grass is. You should hear a trumpet-like screech!

# hadow puppets

another fun thing to do when the weather's
good or during an evening. It's worth taking
ime so that it works really well.

## started

really good idea to make animals or
ters as these can be big and easier to
t than fiddly people.

w your puppets on the card or
k paper and cut them out carefully.

e sticks to the back
he puppets.

need a darkened room and a light,
n wall to make shadows. Put the lamp on
or pointing at the wall and move your
s in front of it: you should see shadows.

can write your own fun mini-play to
form for an audience. Ideally, see if
n do it hiding behind a sofa with the
ws appearing on the wall above!

# Bird feast

Here is an easy and clever way to give the birds in your garden a really nice feast. The best time to feed birds is in winter, especially when the weather is very cold. But you can give them this feast all year round.

## Stuff you need
- **Stiff garden wire (four pieces about 40cm long)**
- An apple
- **An orange**
- Bird seeds
- **A chopping board, knife and spoon**

## Get started

**1** Bend the pieces of wire so they are this shape:

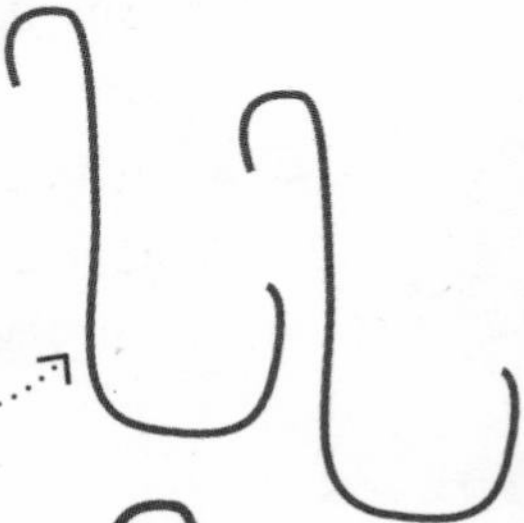

**2** Cut the apple into halves then cut each half into four pieces. Carefully push these onto the bottom of one piece of wire.

**3** Cut the orange in half and carefully scoop out all of the flesh (you can eat this!) leaving two empty skins shaped like little bowls.

**4** Thread the wire through these (one each) as shown here and fill them with bird seed.

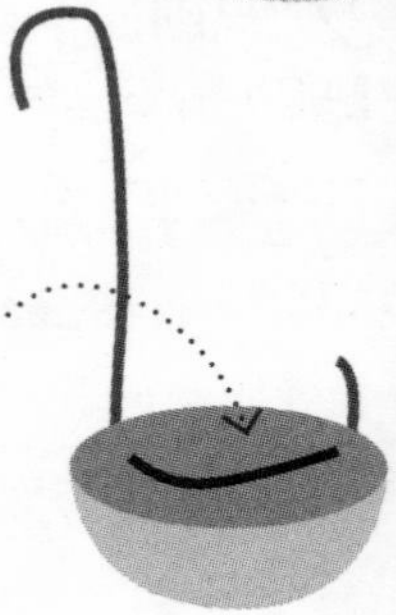

**5** Hang your fruity feeders from a tree and let the birds feast!

# Bird bath

Birds like to have somewhere to drink and wash in summer so why not make them their own bird bath?

## Stuff you need
- A large plant pot saucer (you can buy these at garden centres)
- Three bricks
- Some small pebbles or gravel
- A large stone

## Get started

**1** Find somewhere good to sit the bird bath. Arrange the three bricks on the ground like this:

**2** Place the saucer on the bricks and add the pebbles and stone.

**3** Fill it with water (not right to the top) and it's ready!

**4** Clean and re-fill your bird bath from time to time.

# Lemonade

If you've never had home-made lemonade before then you are in for a treat. It's easy to make and really delicious – one of the best things about summer! Ask an adult before using the hob.

## Stuff you need

- 3 lemons
- Half a cup of sugar
- A cup of water
- A large bottle of sparkling water
- A pan, a jug and a wooden spoon

## Get started

1 Put the fizzy water in the fridge so it's cool.

2 Put the sugar in a pan and add the cup of water. Gently heat this and stir until the sugar dissolves. Leave it to cool then pour it into the jug.

3 Squeeze the lemons and add all of the juice (but no pips) into the jug. Stir well.

4 When the mixture is cool, pour it into glasses so they are one-third full. Top up with the sparkling water. Add ice and a straw if you wish.

# Jokes

Emma: Gemma, will that pizza you're making be long?
Gemma: No, it'll be round.

What's the most dangerous hobby? Pottery – they're always throwing pots.

Dad: Why is that boat you made so small?
Kid: It's a model of a model of the Titanic.

Mum: How's your new coin collecting hobby going?
Kid: Great, I've nearly got enough for an ice cream.

Dad: Who filled this vase full of white powder?
Kid: It was me – I've taken up flour arranging.

Why did the boy give up magic tricks? His hat was full of rabbit poo.

Mum: Why is granny purple?
Kid: You said I could paint her.

47

# PLACES TO GO

Summer is the best time of year to get out and visit some exciting places. This section is full of ideas for places to go, both near and far, and fun things to do there. Some of them could be done locally in a morning or afternoon and others need a full day out. So, start being extra nice to your parents before asking if they'll take you!

# Town: Explore a castle

There is something magical about a real castle, even if it's a ruin. Maybe there's one near you.

## Stuff you need

- A guidebook or leaflet showing what's what in the castle
- A camera

## Get started

1. Finding a good castle to explore is the first part of your quest. The internet has several useful websites to help you.
2. Check whether the castle is open for visits and what dates and times it is open.
3. Explore your chosen castle imagining what it was like to be someone attacking or defending it long ago...

# Pavement art

## Stuff you need

- **Some giant chalks in different colours**
- Something soft to kneel on like an old jumper
- **A camera or smartphone (not essential)**

Drawing on a pavement with chalk can be a great way to pass an hour or two if you can find a good place to do it. Just make sure an adult is with you at all times if you're out on the street.

## Get started

1. First you need to find a quiet, clean pavement:
⊙ Make sure you're well away from traffic and not in the way of pedestrians.
⊙ Smooth paving stones work best (avoid tarmac).
⊙ The ideal place is outside your home, or in a park.
2. Get drawing! Here are some things to try:
❍ Monsters or aliens
❍ Simple animals such as butterflies, fish, snakes or owls
❍ A favourite cartoon character (copy from a printed picture)
❍ Patterns such as spirals, stars, wavy lines, zig-zags and circles
❍ A simple puzzle such as a maze, a small wordsearch or a giant snakes and ladders board
❍ A play mat-style layout with roads for toy cars
❍ Copy a famous painting such as Van Gogh's Sunflowers.
3. You can also make pavement paint by mixing half a cup of cornflour with half a cup of water. Pour the mixture into different containers and add food colouring (about 10 drops) to make your colours.
4. Tips:
⊙ It's easier to work large
⊙ Chalk smudges very easily so avoid kneeling or standing on your pictures
⊙ Take photos of your work: you can't keep it!

*Remember for all of these activities you need an adult with you.

49

# Street photo challenge

This is an entertaining way to find out how well your family knows your town.

## Stuff you need

• **A camera or smartphone** • A notebook and pencil • **A computer or tablet**

## Get started

1. The challenge involves taking lots of photos of places near your home to create a picture quiz for your family or friends. They will try and identify each place from your photos.
• You'll need an adult with you as you need to be out and about on the streets.
• It's best to do this on a day when the weather is good.
• You'll need to take plenty of photos and write down every place you photograph.

2. To make the quiz work well you need to take photos quite close up so that there are not too many clues to give away the locations. Here are some ideas for pictures:
• Parts of street name signs (such as 'Chapel Road')

• Shop windows (remember to write down the name of each shop!)
• Doorways of well-known buildings such as the library, post office or a school
• Part of a statue or monument such as a war memorial
• Wall plaques
• Parts of busy places such as a train station, shopping centre, bus stop or garage
• A well-known building from an unusual angle
• A clock or flag or banner or poster.

3. Load the pictures onto a computer and choose the ten best ones. Crop the images so that they just show enough to make the quiz a little tricky but not too hard! Make sure you have a written list of the answers.

4. Make the finished pictures into a slide show (ask if you're not sure how to do this) and then show them to your quiz audience. You can get them to call out or write down their answers and see who gets the most correct.

**5. One way to make the quiz easier is to make it multiple choice.**

# Follow a town trail walk

Most towns have all kinds of hidden, mysterious and amazing places that people will show you round. You can explore your own town or follow a trail when you're on holiday.

## Get started

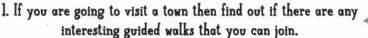

**1. If you are going to visit a town then find out if there are any interesting guided walks that you can join.**

2. If you want to join a guided walk, book in advance if you can or get there early.

**3. If there are no guided walks you fancy, do some online research to see if there's a town trail you can follow. These usually take you to the most interesting places in a town. Download a map if there is one.**

4. You can also visit a town's tourist information centre where they will tell you about the best walks and provide you with maps.

# Park fun

If you have a good park nearby there are all sorts of things you can do there to be un-bored. Here are lots of ideas and possibilities.

## Stuff you need

- Money in case you need to pay for an activity
- Snacks and drinks
- Ball, Frisbee, kite etc, depending on what you decide to do

## Get started

**1. See what the parks in your town have to offer. You might find some or even all of these:**
- Adventure playground
- Mini golf
- Boating pond or lake
- Tennis
- Zip wire
- Trampolines
- Skate zone
- Giant games like draughts or Jenga
- Karting
- Sports coaching.

**2. If your park has lots of open space you can play your own game – here are some ideas:**
- Frisbee golf (put down some targets and see how many throws it takes you to reach them all)
- Rounders (you can play with a small cricket bat and posts)
- Football (or have a penalty shoot-out)
- Cricket (use a tennis ball and get everyone to field)
- Keepy-uppy (stand in a circle and count how many touches you can do to keep the ball up together, two touches each at a time)
- Bike courses (watch out for stray toddlers)
- Skittles (use plastic bottles and a ball)
- Kite-flying (keep away from trees and overhead cables)
- Water pistol challenges (take a big supply of water to refill)
- Catch (can you keep two balls in the air at once?)
- Bubbles (who can blow the biggest?)
- Paper planes (who can fly the furthest)
- Or make up your own game!

**3. If it's a nice summer's day, finish off with a picnic!**

# Street name fun

## Stuff you need

- **Paper and pen**
- Camera or phone (not essential)

Here's another enjoyable thing you can do in a town or city. Just make sure that if you're out on the streets you have an adult with you.

## Get started

**1** Walk around your neighbourhood and write down a list of road names.

**2** Make up some anagrams (where you jumble up the letters of a word) for someone else to solve, for example:

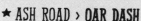

- ★ ASH ROAD › **OAR DASH**
- ★ FAR VIEW CLOSE › **FIVE REAL COWS**

**3** Try changing one letter of street names to make them funny, for example:

- ★ High Street › **Sigh Street**
- ★ Turner's Lane › **Turner's Late**

**4** Cover up part of the road signs with your legs or hands to make them silly, for example:

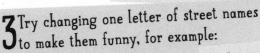

- ★ West Close › **We  lose**
- ★ Myrtle Street › **My   treet**
- ★ Pierce Avenue › **Pie   venue**
- ★ Cowgate › **owgate**
- ★ Francis Hill › **Fran is ill**

# Fun list
## Silly cities

These cities have lost a letter and become a bit sillier. Can you think of any more?

| | |
|---|---|
| Cape Town | **Ape Town** |
| **Kiev** | Kev |
| Hong Kong | **Hog Kong** |
| **Bradford** | Badford |
| Miami | **Mami** |
| **Saint Petersburg** | Aint Petersburg |
| Perth | **Erth** |
| **Sofia** | Sofa |

# Challenge

How many words can you make from the letters of: **WILDLIFE**

⚙ They must contains at least three letters

⚙ No names of people or places are allowed

⚙ Targets:  **10** › **Good**
         **15** › **Excellent**
         **20** › **Amazing**

(You'll find a list of words on page 155)

54

# Woods: go birdwatching

Lots of birds inhabit woods and forests across the UK but they are often shy so it's important to be quiet and still if you want to see them!

## What to look out for

See how many of these birds you can spot – some are common, some are rare:

- → Wood warbler
- → Redstart
- → Nuthatch
- → Goldcrest

- → Woodpecker
- → Hawfinch
- → Sparrowhawk
- → Long-tailed tit

- → Pheasant
- → Siskin
- → Stock dove
- → Wren

## How to spot birds

1. Keep still and hidden as much as possible – stay near a tree trunk.
2. Avoid wearing bright clothing.
3. Use your ears as well as your eyes – listen out for the rapid rattle of a woodpecker, for example.
4. Look up and scan branches with your binoculars.
5. Try not to stand on noisy snapping branches.

# Find animal tracks and signs

The best time to find tracks is when it's been raining and there are patches of mud. You can find other signs at any time – you just need to look very carefully. Here are some clues to search for:

## Animal tracks

Look in places where there are patches of shallow mud.

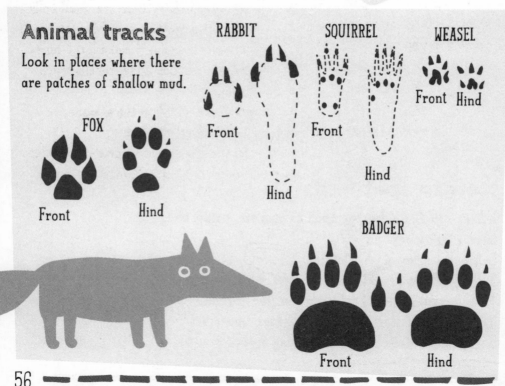

RABBIT
Front
Hind

SQUIRREL
Front
Hind

WEASEL
Front  Hind

FOX
Front    Hind

BADGER
Front      Hind

## Droppings

Yes, searching for poo can tell you a lot! Most animal droppings aren't stinky either.

⊙ **Rabbits and hares** – small round pellets, made up of finely chewed grass.

⊙ **Fox** – like a small dog poo, often twisted at one end.

⊙ **Deer** – large black pellets, pointed at one end.

## Other signs

If you're going to be a smart animal detective then these are all good clues.

❷ **Chewed bark** – rabbits, squirrels and deer do this.

❷ Hairs – badgers often leave black and white hairs on fences.

❷ **Owl pellets** – these are small balls of undigested bones and fur, spat out.

❷ Holes – badgers make large holes of around 30cm wide, rabbits much smaller.

❷ **Nests** – look in thick bushes and hedges.

❷ Food leftovers – for example pine cones stripped by hungry squirrels.

# Make a shelter

This is a real challenge but it's fun to do, and if you can hide in your shelter it may help you to spot more birds and woodland animals. Remember to leave no trace when you go home.

## Stuff you need

- **Long branches and sticks**
- Smaller branches and leafy twigs
- **Leaves**

## How to start

**1** You need three long sticks or branches to start with. One of these needs to have a forked end.

**2** Arrange the branches like this, sticking them into the ground if you can:

**3** Add more long sticks to each side:

**4** Hang smaller leafy branches from the framework on each side, leaving the front open. Add more leaves and branches to cover any gaps. You now have a shelter!

# Leaf art

Forests and woods are full of natural colourful materials that you can use to make collages and other art.

## Stuff you need

- Colourful leaves
- Twigs, pine cones, seeds and other natural objects
- A camera or phone to take pictures

## Get started

1 First, find a good surface to work on: some short grass, a flat tree stump or a quiet path.

2 Start arranging your leaves into interesting patterns – think about shape, colour and contrast. Here are some ideas:

3 You can also use leaves and twigs to make collages of animals:

# Ride a forest bike trail

There are bike trails in woods and forests all over the country and they are good fun to ride on. Just remember to be prepared for mud and all sorts of weather!

## Get started

1. The first thing to do is some research. Use the internet to find out where there are bike trails near you. For example, if you live in Kent, type into a search engine, 'forest bike trails Kent'.

2. You can either take your own bikes if your parents/carers have a way to transport them, or you may be able to hire bikes at the location.

3. Decide how far to ride. Pick an easy route first and see what it's like. Stick together and wear a helmet: some forest rides have lumpy tree roots and steep hills!

## Stuff you need

- Bikes and helmets
- A map of the trails – you can usually get these at visitor centres
- A water bottle each

# Jokes

## Tree tee-hee

| | |
|---|---|
| Which tree loves sunbathing? | A beech |
| Which tree is green and juicy? | A lime |
| Which tree is always warm? | A fir |
| Which tree is square? | A box |
| Which tree is retired? | An elder |
| Which always grows in twos? | A pear |
| Which tree isn't me? | A yew |

## Town test

Each answer is a town or city...

| | |
|---|---|
| Where's the best place to get wet? | Bath |
| Where's the best place to wander about? | Rome |
| Where's the best place to take zombies? | Bury |
| Where's the best place to get some boots? | Wellington |
| Where's the best place to hear a growl? | Lyon |
| Where's the best place to buy Christmas table decorations? | Caracas |
| Where's the best place to have a good time? | Nice |
| Where's the best place to walk your dog? | Leeds |
| Where's the best place to buy a useless car? | Bangor |
| Where's the best place to seal a bottle? | Cork |

# Rivers: play Pooh sticks

## Stuff you need
- Some short sticks or twigs
- A river or stream
- A bridge

Pooh sticks is the classic river game, as played by Winnie the Pooh and his friends. Believe it or not, it's a proper sport with rules and a World Championships!

## Get started

**1** Pooh sticks can be played by two or more people – each person needs a stick.

**2** Stand on the side of the bridge with the water flowing towards you. Don't pick a busy bridge used by traffic (a footbridge is best).

**3** Each person holds out their stick, the oldest person says, 'Ready, steady, go' and everyone drops their stick at the same time.

**4** The winner is the person whose stick appears first on the other side of the bridge.

**5** Water usually flows faster in some parts of rivers than others. Can you work out how to discover where the fastest flow is?

# Race leaves

Racing leaves on a stream is a good giggle. People usually get wet so it's wise not to wear your Sunday best. Remember that you need an adult with you whenever you're near water!

## Stuff you need

- Leaves of different shapes and colours
- A shallow stream (one you can safely stand in with wellies)
- Wellies

## Get started

1. You do need the right kind of stream to play this game: it should be small and shallow just in case someone falls in. Keep away from fast-flowing or deep water.

2. Decide on a starting point (a bridge is good for this) and a finishing point.

3. Each person should choose a leaf of a different colour.

4. Drop them in the water on the count of three.

5. The winner is the person whose leaf reaches the finish first.

# Follow a stream

Following a stream can be an enjoyable adventure. Make sure you go with adults you know and that you are dressed to get wet!

## Get started

**1** The best kind of stream for this is a small stream in a hilly area. These are usually more interesting than streams flowing through flat country.

**2** Find somewhere such as a forest park or moorland where you are allowed to wander.

**3** The stream needs to be small and shallow so that if you fall in you can easily stand up. Avoid deep and fast-flowing water.

**4** Follow the stream up water and watch out for wildlife: fish, birds such as dippers, and animals such as water voles.

## Stuff you need

- Wellies and waterproofs
- A shallow stream (one you can safely stand in with wellies)

# Talk ?

Here are some fun questions to discuss with friends or family:

What's the best wild place you've ever visited? And the worst?

What would you be like as a farmer?

If you could choose anyone famous to go on a long walk with, who would you choose and why?

# Choose

What would you rather see in the wild:

A weasel **or** a lizard?
A deer **or** a fox?
An owl **or** a badger?
A kingfisher **or** an otter?
A snake **or** an eagle?
A wolf **or** a bear?

# Countryside: see shooting stars

Shooting stars or meteors are a wonderful sight in the night sky, but you need to be in the right place at the right time to see them.

## Get started

**1** The best meteor showers appear at night at these times of the year. These are rough dates for every year – find out the exact dates for this year online. What you can see depends on where in the world you live, so check the list carefully!

| WHAT | WHEN | WHERE |
|---|---|---|
| Quadrantids | peak around Jan 3rd–4th | northern hemisphere only |
| Lyrids | Apr 16th–26th | worldwide |
| Eta Aquariids | peak around May 5th–6th | best in southern hemisphere |
| Delta Aquariids | peak around July 28–29th | best in southern hemisphere |
| Perseids | peak around Aug 11th–13th | best in northern hemisphere |
| Draconids | peak around Oct 7th–8th | best in northern hemisphere |
| Orionids | peak around Oct 21st–22nd | worldwide |
| South Taurids | peak around Nov 4th–5th | worldwide |
| North Taurids | peak around Nov 11th–12th | worldwide |
| Leonids | peak around Nov 17th–18th | worldwide |
| Geminids | peak around Dec 13th 14th | worldwide |
| Ursids | peak around Dec 21st–22nd | northern hemisphere only |

**2** You can't see shooting stars on cloudy nights or in towns and cities where there is a lot of light pollution.

Shooting stars are rapid streaks of light caused by particles of rock burning in the Earth's atmosphere.

**3** The best thing is to check the weather forecast for clear skies on one of the above dates then ask at home if you can be taken on a night-time trip into the countryside to look for meteors.

**4** Wrap up warm and just keep staring up at the sky!

# Spot constellations

Star watching on a clear night in the country, away from light pollution, is a most excellent thing to do – especially in the summer when it's hopefully not too cold.

## Get started

1 Check the weather forecast for clear skies then ask at home if someone can take you star watching.

2 Not all constellations are visible all year, and also which ones you can see depends on whether you are standing in the northern or southern hemisphere.

Here are some constellations to look out for in the summer:

✳ **The Great Bear (Ursa Major)** – northern hemisphere
✳ **The Little Bear (Ursa Minor)** – northern hemisphere

## Stuff you need

• **Warm clothing**
• A good weather forecast!
• Binoculars
• **A guide to the night sky showing constellations of stars**

✳ **The Queen (Cassiopeia)** – northern hemisphere
✳ **The Swan (Cygnus)** – both hemispheres
✳ **The Scorpion (Scorpius)** – both hemispheres
✳ **Crux (Southern Cross)** – southern hemisphere

3 Use a book or a phone app to check you are looking in the right place!

# Go geocaching

## Stuff you need

- A handheld GPS device (or smartphone with geocaching app)
- A small item of 'treasure' (a trinket or something useful)
- A computer with internet access
- A parent for help and transport

If you like the idea of treasure hunting then you'll love geocaching. This is like a hi-tech treasure hunt. You use GPS (satellite navigation) technology to search for and find hidden boxes containing all sorts of things – and you can do it anywhere in the world.

## Get started

1. Visit www.geocaching.com to find a cache (hidden box) in the countryside near you – this website also explains more about how geocaching works.

2. Pick a cache to find then enter the co-ordinates in your GPS device.

3. The GPS will take you towards the cache but you'll have to find it!

4. A cache is a plastic box with a lid – inside you'll find a logbook which you can fill in.

5. You might also find a bit of treasure in the box – remember that if you take something you should put something else back in the box for the next person to find.

6. Return the cache carefully and choose your next one.

# Use a map and compass to find a location

Being able to use a map and compass is a really useful skill and it's fun too – provided you don't end up in a squelchy bog...

## Get started

**1** Get hold of a really good map. By far the best maps of Great Britain, for example, are the OS 1:25,000 Explorer series – these have lots of useful detail.

**2** The first job is to locate where you are – make sure you get it right!

**3** Next, look on the map for an interesting location 1-2km away (each square on the map is one kilometre): it should be by a road or footpath.

**4** Work out the route to get there and note which direction you need to head in first (north is at the top of the map).

**5** Use the compass to find the right direction and keep checking the map. Use the compass each time you change direction.

# Visit a farm

There are lots of farms you can visit to pet piglets, feed lambs, enjoy tractor rides and explore maize mazes.

## Stuff you need

- Wellies and suitable clothes
- Something to eat and drink

## Get started

1. The first job is to find a farm nearby which welcomes visitors. A good way to do this is with a web search – for example, type 'farms to visit in [your area]' into a search engine.
2. Decide on a farm and choose the kinds of activities you want to do. Farms with animals tend to be more muddy.
3. Get there early so you don't miss out on activities which are at set times.
4. Entertain each other on the way with some farm jokes like these:

Why was the farmer successful?
She was outstanding in her field.

What's a horse's favourite sport?
Stable tennis.

Why didn't the farmer watch the film about tractors?
The trailer wasn't very good.

What's a sheep's favourite manoeuvre?
A ewe-turn.

Is chicken soup good for you?
Not if you're the chicken.

72

# Pick fruit

Mid summer is a great time to pick strawberries and raspberries and other yummy fruit.

## Stuff you need

- Old clothes (in case they get stained with juice)
- A drink

## Get started

**1** If you have soft fruit at home in the garden then make sure you ask permission before picking it!

**2** Pick ripe fruit only – berries that are soft and dark.

**3** Never eat a berry unless you know what it is!

**4** If you don't have any soft fruit in your garden, ask if you can go to a 'pick your own' farm. Here you can pick lots of raspberries or strawberries but you do have to pay for them!

# Make natural paints

Painting is good, but actually making your own paints from things in the countryside and then painting with them is *really* good.

## Get started

1. This is a very messy activity so wear old clothes or an apron.

2. Look for your ingredients:
- Chalk rock to make white
- Ash or burnt wood to make grey and black
- Leaves to make green
- Berries (e.g. elderberries or blackberries) to make red and purple
- Flower petals to make yellow or blue
- Clay to make brown.

3. Crush the chalk or ash or burnt wood in the pestle to make a powder, then add a little water.

4. Soft berries can be squashed through a sieve.

5. Leaves and petals may have to be crushed with the pestle and mortar.

6. Add a little water to each colour as needed, then try painting patterns on paper, stones or wood.

# Score

Give these days out a rating of A, B, C, D or E:

A walk up a windy mountain

A visit to a remote castle

A boat trip along a river

Camping by the sea

Feeding animals on a farm

A day at a karting track

Exploring an air museum

Rock climbing

Gathering wild fruit in a forest

# Love, hate or meh?

The countryside isn't for everyone – how do you rate these? Give these outdoor things a score out of ten.

Mud     Cowpats     Butterflies     Woodlands     Hills

Tractors     Nettles     Birds     Farms     Bulls

# Pond: try pond dipping

Ponds are mini-worlds of fascinating wildlife and one of the best ways to see it is to go pond dipping. Make sure you ask permission first, and remember to stay away from deep water at all times and be careful at the edge of ponds.

## Stuff you need

- A net or sieve
- A white tray (or a baking tray with white paper in it)
- A plastic container
- Wellies

## Get started

1. Be quiet and still near the pond so you don't disturb creatures.
2. Scoop up some pond water with the plastic container and put it in your tray.
3. Lower your net into the water and move it around carefully, then place it in the tray so what you catch can be emptied out. Don't lean too far!

4. A sieve is good for dipping at the pond's edge among the plants – lots of water life hides here.
5. You can identify your catches with a magnifying glass and a book or a guide sheet (you can download these from the web and print them). Put everything back in the pond at the end.

# Make a pond viewer

Here is a sneaky way to actually look into a pond and see the little water creatures (or maybe even big ones) that lie beneath the surface.

## Get started

1 Take the lid off the bottle and squash it flat (the bottle, not the lid!).

2 With the scissors, cut a slit in the bottle about 10cm from the top, as in the picture. Take care as the cut edges will be sharp.

3 Pop the bottle back into shape, then, using the slit, carefully cut a long rectangle out of the side of the bottle so that you have a viewing window about 20cm long and 10cm wide.

4 Put tape over the sharp edges and your viewer is ready!

5 Lie down with just your head over the pond so you can't fall in, and lower your viewer into the water with the window side up. Hopefully, you'll see all sorts of wonders.

77

# Find tadpoles

Everyone knows that tadpoles turn into frogs and toads but not everyone gets the chance to catch some and watch them up close. Here's how.

## Stuff you need
- A fine-mesh net or sieve attached to a stick
- Large glass jar
- Magnifying glass

## Get started

1. You need to do this in spring or you might be too late!

2. First, half-fill your jar with water from the pond.

3. At the pond, look for clumps of jelly-like frogspawn. If you find some, carefully scoop it up with the net and put it in the water.

4. You can also catch tadpoles among the weeds and pop them in the container water.

5. Look at them up close and see how amazing they are.

6. Put the tadpoles back in the pond after about ten minutes or so.

# Lake: skimming stones

Skimming stones is one of life's simple joys but you need to know a few things if you want to do it well.

## Stuff you need

- Rounded, flat stones or pebbles
- A lake or river with a small beach

## Get started

1 It's definitely best to collect good stones before you go skimming – when you get to a suitable watery spot you'll find that all the good stones have gone! The best place to collect skimming stones is on beaches but you can also find them by rivers flowing through hills.

2 Skimming is almost impossible if the water is choppy and even small ripples and waves can make it difficult, which is why trying to skim stones in the sea rarely works! Evening is the best time, when the wind tends to die down and the water is calm.

3 Find a lake with a long clear stretch of water next to a small beach – you need to be low down near the water level to skim well.

4 Choose a stone you can wrap your index finger half way round. Bend your knees with legs slightly apart and throw the stone with a wristy flicking action – you are aiming to spin the stone with your finger as you release it.

5 Count how many hops you can do!

# Sail a model boat or raft

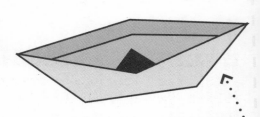

Making your own model boat is a real challenge and making one that floats is even harder! But give it a try because you might be brilliant!

## Stuff you need

- **Paper** (for a paper boat)
- Sticks and string (for a model raft)

## To make a paper boat

1. Fold the paper in half along its length.

2. Open it out then fold it in half the other way.

3. Fold the two closed corners down to the centre line.

4. Fold up the bottom edges on both sides.

**5. Put your thumbs inside and pull apart the middle then flatten the shape so it's square.**

6. Fold the front and back layers up on each side as shown.

**7. Again put your thumbs inside the shape, pull out the middle and flatten.**

8. Your shape needs to be the same way round as the picture. Pull the two pointed tips apart.

**9. Flatten the bottom and pull the sides up.**

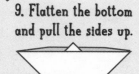

10. Open out the inside a little and you have a paper boat with a sail!

# To make a raft

1. You'll need about 15 sticks around 18-20cm long (straight twigs will do).

2. Put two sticks down crossways and lie 8-10 sticks on top as shown. Make sure that the ends of the two bottom twigs are sticking out.

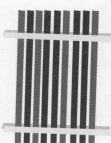

3. Now lie two more sticks on top, level with the two at the bottom.

4. Join the four cross-sticks at each end tightly with rubber bands.

5. To make the 8-10 sticks more secure, weave string around their ends (over one then under the next then back again). Do this twice at each end and tie the string so it can't come undone.

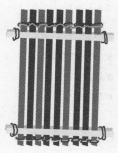

6. Test your raft to find out if it floats. See if you can work out how to add a mast and a paper sail.

## More tips

- There are lots of excellent videos on the internet that show you how to make paper boats and model rafts.
- In a search engine type 'make a paper boat video' and look at a few of the results. Pause the video as you go along, copying it.
- Try out your boat on a lake or shallow stream. Remember to stay away from deep water.

# Hills: eat up a mountain

Climbing a big hill or mountain is a great achievement but even better is rewarding yourself with a mini-feast at the top!

## Get started

**1** The first thing is to ask a nice friendly adult you know to take you to some hills or mountains.

**2** Plan a route along a footpath using a map. Remember that if you've never walked up hills before it's very tiring!

**3** Prepare your feast: sandwiches, fruit, choc bars and things that are easy to carry. Remember to take lots of drinks – climbing makes you thirsty.

**4** Conquer your peak!

## Stuff you need

- A map of where you are going
- Food and plenty of water to drink
- Suitable clothing in case it rains (it rains a lot on mountains)
- Good strong shoes (walking boots are best; flips flops are a no-no)

# Hillside art

Oh, this is good. If you didn't know that you can make giant works of art on hillsides, read on...

## Get started

1 Hillside art involves using stones and rocks found on hillsides to create large-scale pictures on the ground. You can also spell out messages.

2 The hardest part is finding somewhere you can do this. It needs to be:
- ☞ **A hilly place with open areas of short grass**
- ☞ Somewhere with small valleys and dips
- ☞ **Somewhere there are rocks and stones lying about.**

3 Explore footpaths up hillsides, looking for an open grassy place in a dip or small valley.

4 Start collecting stones (light-coloured ones show up best against the hilly background).

5 Create a big picture using the stones on the grass – if you can, do it in a place where you can get a good photo looking down.

## Stuff you need
- Suitable clothes in case it rains
- Drinks and snacks
- A strong bag to collect stones

83

# Indoors: indoor coconut shy

This is a way to enjoy fairground fun without the expense or the travelling. And you can have as many goes as you like!

## Get started

1. The first thing is to choose a room or space where nothing will get knocked over or broken by flying balls of paper.

2. Next, make the three stands for the coconuts: simply roll the A4 paper into tubes longways, so they are about the width of toilet roll tubes. Tape them so they can't come undone.

3. The 'coconuts' are made from scrunched-up newspaper. Tape two sheets of newspaper together to make a really big sheet, then scrunch this up into a large ball. Wrap some tape around it to stop it coming undone. Do three of these and balance them on top of the tubes.

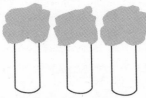

4. Next make the paper balls to throw: each one is made by scrunching up tight half a sheet of newspaper. Make as many of these as you like – at least 5-6 for each person.

5. You're ready to play! Set the coconuts up just in front of a wall (either on the floor or on a low table) then choose a throwing line to stand or sit on and start hurling!

# Sock juggling

Juggling with tennis balls is best done outdoors but if it's a rainy day you can always try juggling indoors with socks...

## Stuff you need

• Two pairs of socks

## Get started

1. The socks need to be rolled up first: put your thumbs into each sock and fold over the top. Keep doing this until each sock is rolled into a nice tight ball.

2. Find a space indoors where you won't knock anything over or get in anyone's way.

3. Try out a little throwing and catching with each hand first. Throw a sock from your left to your right hand and back again.

4. Another good juggling practice is to try and throw and catch two socks in the same hand. When one is in the air, throw the other one straight up gently. It takes a lot of patience, but keep trying.

5. Try juggling with two socks in two hands next: simply throw one up with your best hand then pass the other sock to it. Catch the first sock with the weaker hand and keep doing this so that the socks are circling.

6. Three socks is MUCH harder, so don't be too disappointed if you really struggle or can't do it at all. The best way to learn is to start with two socks in your best hand and one in your other hand.

• Throw one from your best hand over to the other hand.

• As that sock is in the air you need to throw the one from your weaker hand the other way so the two cross over.

• Then, of course you need to throw the third sock across before the second one lands!

• The secret is to use a nice steady rhythm of throws.

## Tips

• Ask someone who can juggle to patiently show you.

• Watch some 'how to juggle' videos on the internet.

• Don't give up when you drop the balls – you just have to keep trying until you've got it.

# Draw an impossible triangle

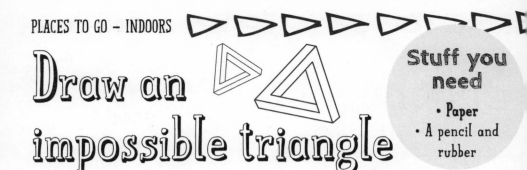

## Stuff you need

- **Paper**
- A pencil and rubber

You've probably seen pictures before of these 'impossible' 3-D shapes which cannot be made. But they can be drawn – and here's how to do one.

## Get started

Follow the steps below. Each new line to draw is shown in grey. Dotted lines need to be rubbed out.

*You can use a ruler – it's not cheating!*

*Press lightly with your pencil so rubbing out is easy.*

*Draw fair large.*

# Balloon volleyball

This is a very simple game that can be played inside by two people. You will need a little bit of space and to avoid things like vases, babies, lamps, cats, laptops...

## Stuff you need

- **A balloon**
- A light sheet
- **Some clothes pegs**
- String

## Get started

**1** Volleyball involves a net, so the first job is to make a net using the sheet. One idea is to peg it to the top of two dining chairs placed across the room. Or it could be draped over some soft furniture in the middle. The net should be as high as possible.

**2** One person stands on each side of the net. You'll need to decide your playing area (volleyball pitch) – this can be marked out with string. It should be the same size on each side of the court.

**3** The aim of the game is very simple: hit the balloon over the net with your hand and try and get the other person to miss the court when they hit the balloon back. If the balloon lands outside the court (or on the wrong side of the net), that's a point to the other person. A player can also win a point by hitting a balloon onto the other person's side of the court.

**4** Take turns to serve from the back of the court. The first player to ten wins. After that you can swap ends.

# Test your reaction times

How fast are you at reacting to things? Here's a sneaky and fascinating way to measure your reaction times.

## Stuff you need

- **A 30cm ruler**
- Pen and paper
- **A calculator (not essential)**

## Get started

**1** You need two people for this: one to be tested (the catcher) and one to do the testing (the dropper).

**2** The catcher needs to sit on a chair resting his or her arm on a table. The catcher's hand needs to be positioned so it's just off the table.

**3** The catcher opens his or her hand, keeping the fingers together, so that the thumb and fingers are 5cm apart (the dropper measures this with the ruler).

**4** The dropper then places the zero end of the ruler in this gap and then drops it after a few seconds. The catcher has to try and catch the ruler right away.

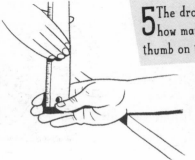

**5** The dropper can measure the catcher's reaction time by seeing how many centimetres are marked by the top of the catcher's thumb on the ruler. Write this down, then repeat five times.

**6** To get a score for the catcher, add up the five scores and divide by five to find an average.

**7** Swap over so that the dropper now becomes the catcher. Test, measure and compare! Can you beat your parents or your friends?

# Hear a sci-fi laser battle

This is cool, amazing, unexpected, strange, fun, and very easy to do. What are you waiting for?

## Get started

1. Slinky springs are fun to play with but few people know that they make an amazing sound too.

2. To hear the sound, hold a slinky at the very top and let it dangle. Push your index finger through the second coil of the spring at the top so that the slinky is dangling from one finger.

3. Keeping your finger straight, put it into one ear — you should be able to hear strange sounds.

4. Keeping the slinky dangling from the finger in your ear, try moving around a little so the slinky swings. Bend down so that the slinky hits the ground while you listen (a hard floor works best).

5. Ask someone to tap the slinky gently with a spoon while you listen — you should hear some weird 'laser battle' sounds!

6. Experiment and see what else affects the sound. You can hear the sound without a finger in your ear by pushing a paper cup into the top of the slinky, holding the slinky around the cup and letting the rest of the spring drop.

# Make a mini-rocket

Here's a brilliant little making project which is quite quick, easy and gives excellent results. We have lift-off!

## Stuff you need

- **Paper and pencil**
- Ruler
- A plastic drinking straw
- Scissors
- **Sticky tape**
- Crayons or felt pens (not essential)

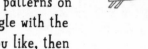

## Get started

**1** Start by marking out a rectangle, which is 10cm long and 5cm wide, in the corner of the paper.

**2** Draw some patterns on the rectangle with the crayons if you like, then cut it out.

**3** Place the pencil along the long edge of your rectangle then roll the paper rectangle tightly around the pencil to make a paper tube.

**4** Tape the paper tube so it can't come undone (don't tape it to the pencil!).

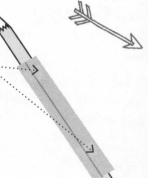

**5** Take the pencil out and flatten one end of the tube. Fold over the two corners and tape these down. This is the top of the rocket.

**6** The rocket needs fins to fly well, so draw this whole shape on the paper then cut it out:

**7** Tape the piece with the fins to the bottom of the rocket so that the fins stick out.

**8** Place the rocket on the straw, point it upwards and blow hard. It should fly!

straw

**9** Experiment to find ways to improve the rocket. Try different fins or a different nose shape (the top of the tube must be closed so the air can't escape) or try different lengths and sizes. You can also add some stylish design touches.

91

# AT THE BEACH

Ah, the seaside: stinging jellyfish, sand in your eyes, freezing cold water, slimy seaweed and cloudy skies — and those are just the fun bits! Not really, of course! The seaside is a magical place to have fun in summer and this section of the book has oodles of ideas for how to make the most of it.

## Talk

These are fun to chat about on the way to the beach

- What's your favourite beach?
- **What's your top beach activity?**
- What's the funniest thing you've ever seen at the seaside?
- **Is there anything you don't like about beaches? Why?**

## Choose

Pebble beach or sandy beach?
**Busy beach or empty beach?**
Hot sun or cool breeze?
**Big waves or calm water?**
Rock pooling or building sandcastles?
**Splashing in the sea or sunbathing?**
Finding fossils or finding crabs?

## Beach favourites

What will you do when you get there? Here are some excellent traditional activities:

- Build a sandcastle
- Dig a giant hole
- Make a dam
- Create a sand boat to sit in
- Build a sand pyramid
- Make a helter-skelter track for a ball (around a mound)
- Fly a kite

# Hunt for fossils

It's very cool and exciting to discover a once-living creature millions of years old that has turned to stone. Here's how to do it...

## Stuff you need

- A bag for interesting finds
- A fossil book (not essential)
- A camera (not essential)

## Get started

1. First you need to know where to look for fossils. The seaside is an excellent place because the sea wears away the coast and keeps turning up fossils that were once hidden. Do a bit of research to find out the best fossil-hunting places near you.

2. It's very important to stay away from cliffs when you are looking for fossils by the sea. Sea cliffs are often crumbly and can collapse dangerously. Good places to look are:

- On the beach when the tide is going out
- Among the shingle (small pebbles) on stony beaches
- Under rocks
- In small streams.

3. It's all right to pick up small loose fossils but don't try and remove a fossil that is part of a large rock. Don't use a hammer either – you'll end up hurting yourself and the fossil!

# Beachcombing

Beachcombing is searching for interesting finds along a beach. It's amazing what you can find, especially after a storm.

## Stuff you need

• A bag or bucket for interesting finds

## Get started

**1** First you need a beach!

**2** Top tips for finding beach treasure:
a) Winter is a good time to look, when rough seas wash up all sorts of things.
b) Try and search when the tide is going out.
c) Start early in the day – before other people!
d) Search among rocks, seaweed and groynes.
e) Don't take any living creatures.

**3** How many of these can you find?

• Shells
• Sea sponges
• Crab claws
• Sea urchins
• Fossils
• Shark eggs

• Fish skeletons
• Driftwood
• Sea-smoothed glass
• Pottery fragments
• Buttons
• Coins

• Amber
• Jet
• Flotsam and jetsam (things washed up from boats)

# Make a pebble tower

Sandy beaches are good but stony beaches have their own kind of magic. Here's a good way to enjoy them.

## Stuff you need

- Plenty of pebbles
- A camera (optional)

## Get started

**1. A good place to start is to find a large, flat rock on the beach to act as the base for your tower.**

2. Next, pick a few larger stones (no bigger than your fist) and start to build with them, turning and twisting until you find the sturdiest way for them to balance, one on top of the other.

**3. Keep adding pebbles, making them smaller as you go.**

4. There are all sorts of challenges to try:
- Who can make the tallest tower?
- Can you balance 10 pebbles on each other?
- Can you make an unusual or special construction?

**5. If the pebbles are very round and hard to balance then you can wedge small thin stones between them to make them stable.**

6. Take photos of your towers – you'll have to leave them behind for others to admire!

# Best pebble competition

This is a contest that anyone can win — so get down to the beach right now!

## Stuff you need

- Bags or a bucket
- A person to be the judge
- Some small prizes

## Get started

1. The simplest way to do this is to let everyone search part of the beach and then choose their best three pebbles to enter into the final — the judge picks winners and runners up.

2. To make it more fun, you can have different categories:
- Prettiest pebble
- Most interesting pebble
- Best 'non-rock' pebble (the sea will smooth anything into flat round shapes including coal, wood, plastic, leather, rubber, brick, glass and bone)
- Best sea glass or pottery fragment
- Best non-pebble find (shell, skeleton piece, seaweed, fossil or mystery item).

3. See if you can identify some of your pebbles using a rock collectors' book. Here are some common rocks:

Granite — speckled and very hard
Sandstone — softer with lines or layers
Quartz — usually milky white (although it can be almost any colour!)
Slate — flat and grey
Flint — smooth and looks like broken glass if it's broken.

# Paint pebbles

Everyone should have a go at painting a pebble at some time in their life. What are you waiting for?

## Get started

**1** Acrylic paints are good because they are quick-drying and the brushes clean in water. Just remember to cover any surface you are working on with a plastic sheet or old newspapers first!

**2** You can paint patterns or pictures directly onto very light or very dark pebbles but many grey pebbles may be best painted white or a bright colour first then left to dry before adding detail.

**3** What to paint? Here are some ideas:

## Stuff you need

- 3 or 4 smooth, plain pebbles (very dark or very light ones work well)
- Acrylic paints and brushes
- **Pots and old dishes**
- A plastic sheet or newspapers
- Old clothes to wear

### TIPS FOR SUCCESS:
- Use a fine brush for detail
- Let one colour dry before painting another one over or next to it
- Practise on paper first (or sketch the design)
- For very fine detail you can use a fine-tipped permanent marker pen

**a) Patterns – simple is often best!**
- Dots
- Lines
- Swirls
- Spirals
- Zig zags

**b) Animals that fit well into a rounded pebble shape:**
- Ladybirds
- Owls
- Bees
- Fish

**c) Other ideas:**
- Monsters
- Funny faces
- Letters of the alphabet

# Jump waves

The sea is always cold when you first stand in it, but you get used to it. Remember, you need a sandy beach to jump waves, not a steep, rocky one!

## Get started

## Stuff you need

- A safe, sandy beach
- Swimming costume (or bare feet and shorts)
- Towels

1 Stand ankle-deep in the water until you are used to it. When you are, jump over the waves as they come in.

2 Jumping waves is best done at high tide or as the tide is going out. Stay near an adult you know and don't go too deep into the water.

3 Try hopping on each foot – can you do it without stumbling?

4 Running along the sand at top speed through the very shallowest water is also fun!

# Swim in the sea

Swimming in the sea can be brilliant fun, and totally different from swimming laps in your local pool. Make sure you follow the golden rules below to keep safe. Only swim in the sea if you have already learned to swim and you can go with a trusted adult.

## Stuff you need

- A safe, sandy beach with lifeguards on duty
- Swimming costume
- Towels
- Warm clothes to change into

## Get started

**1. You need to be able to swim at least 25m, so if you are a learner swimmer it's not safe to try sea swimming yet (stick to paddling).**

2. Only try sea swimming in the summer months – it's too cold and dangerous for children at other times.

**3. The most important thing is to choose the right beach:**
- Find a safe, sandy beach with a lifeguard.
- ONLY SWIM BETWEEN THE TWO RED AND YELLOW FLAGS – these are the safe areas to swim.
- Never swim where there is a red flag or a chequered flag (black and white).

4. Stay near the adult who is with you and only swim where you can put your feet down. Swim along the direction of the shore, not out to sea.

**5. Avoid windy days where there are big waves. Also avoid inflatable toys as these can be blown out to sea.**

6. You will probably get used to the cold but if you stay cold then run back to the beach and get dry and into some warm clothes!

# Go rock pooling

Rock pooling is one of the classic things to do on the beach — who knows what mysterious creatures you might find? It's best to be well prepared, though, and here's how.

## Stuff you need

- **A bucket (a clear one is best)**
- Shoes with a good grip (not flip flops – rocks can be slippery)
- **Hats and sun cream for sun protection**

### Creatures to look out for

- Blenny (fish)
- Shrimp
- Starfish
- Crab
- Goby (fish)
- Sea slugs
- Sea snails
- Mussels
- Sea anemones
- Sponges
- Limpets

## Get started

1. A calm day is best for rock pooling. You need to find a good rocky beach, not a sandy one!

2. Aim to go when the tide is out because you usually find more creatures at the sea edge. Make sure an adult is with you at all times.

3. Use your hands to turn over seaweed and rocks — many creatures love to hide under things. Scoop up some water with a bucket but avoid nets because they can damage delicate animals.

4. Use a spotter's guide to identify your finds. Remember to put back everything you collect.

# Roll down a sand dune

Just remember that if you roll down a sand dune you are going to get very, very, very sandy — so don't do it in your posh suit and tie.

## Stuff you need

- **A beach with sand dunes**

## Get started

**1** Some beaches have sand dunes and some don't, so the first thing you need to do is some research to find out if there is a beach with sand dunes near you. Use a web search engine and you should be able to find one.

**2** Sand dunes are hard to climb and you need to watch out for spiky grass on some of them, but once you are near the top you can have the fun of rolling down. Wheeee!

**3** Here are some other things to try:
- Race to the top (very hard going)
- Run down (massive fun)
- Jump off the top (with a suitable holler)
- Slide down (bare feet work best)
- See how many ways you can roll down.

## Love, hate or meh?
Give these a seaside score out of ten:

Jellyfish    Ice cream    Seagulls    Beachcombing

Sand sculpting    Beach cricket    Body boarding

Climbing sand dunes    Swimming in the sea

# Game

See how many fish puns like these you can come up with:

On your pike!

Nice plaice you've got here.

Can you lend me sick squid?

Did salmon say something?

Pardon, I'm very hard of herring.

Eel never give you any money.

# Jokes

## Watery wit

**What do sea monsters eat?**
Fish and ships.

**Why does it take pirates so long to learn the alphabet?**
Because they spend years at C.

**Why did the crab laugh?**
Because the seaweed.

**Why don't oysters give to charity?**
They're shellfish.

**What does the ocean do when it sees a surfer?**
Waves.

**Who won when the sea and the wind had a race?**
They tide for first place.

**What's the best month to go to the beach?**
Sand June.

## Starfishiness

Which rockpool creature is a celeb?
**A starfish**

Which rockpool creature is in a band?
**A guitarfish**

Which rockpool creature is yummy?
**A choccybarfish**

Which rockpool creature has wheels?
**A carfish**

Which rockpool creature is never near?
**A farfish**

Which rockpool creature likes jam?
**A jarfish**

# Create a beach maze

## Stuff you need

- **A sandy beach**
- A spade (a metal one is best) or a stick

This is loads of fun on a big sandy beach because you can make the maze as enormous and complicated as you like. It doesn't work on a pebble beach, remember!

## Get started

This really only works where you have a sandy beach and the tide is out so that there is a broad flat area of damp sand to draw your maze on.

**1** The first thing to do is to make sure you know how mazes work. They always have:

- **A start**
- **A finish**
- **Lots of different paths to take**
- **Some dead ends**

Typical mazes look like these:

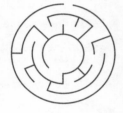

But a maze can be any shape you like!

**2** Draw your maze in the sand, making it large enough for people to walk around. Mark the finish with a stick or rock or something else. Make sure it works!

**3** Invite people to have a go.

# Stone art

Rocky or pebble beaches are fantastic places to collect interesting rocks and to make art with them, especially if there are patches of sand as well. Here are some ideas that rock!

## Stuff you need

- A rocky or pebbly beach
- A bucket or bag to collect pebbles in
- A camera or phone

## Get started

1. The first thing to do is to explore the beach well so that you get an idea of the types of rocks and pebbles to be found.

2. Decide what kind of picture you want to create then collect the right pebbles for it (rather than just collecting loads of rocks you like).

3. Try out some simple ideas, experimenting as you go:
- Lines of graduated sizes or colours work well
- Arrange pebbles in spirals or circles, testing different patterns and colours
- If you want to create an animal, stick to simple shapes such as fish or birds. Snakes or long twisty worms look good
- You can make a mosaic with small coloured stones
- Combine pebbles with sticks if you want lines
- You get a pleasing effect by arranging large smooth stones among tightly packed small pebbles
- Try some shell art.

## Tips

- Make your pebble art on smooth sand if possible
- Keep it simple
- Take photos – you usually can't take pebble art home!

# Sand art

Here are lots of ideas for creating big, bold artworks on the beach. And if they go wrong you just rub 'em out!

## Get started

The best beach for sand art is a large, empty sandy beach where the tide is out. Damp sand is really essential for most of the ideas below.

Try some of these ideas:

## Stuff you need

- A spade (a long-handled metal one is the best)
- A bucket or carrier bag
- Sticks
- **Shells, pebbles, seaweed**

### SAND DRAWING
- You need a large, flat area of damp sand.
- Use the corner of a metal spade to draw with – this gives a lovely clean line (sticks can be used but are not as good).
- Work on a large scale with big sweeping lines.
- Experiment with patterns and shapes as well as drawing familiar things.

### SAND PAINTING
- You need a bag of dry sand from the top of the beach (a sock also works as something to carry sand in!).
- Go onto the darker damp sand and 'paint' by pouring the light, dry sand on top.
- It does not give a clean line but does give nice ghostly effects.

## SAND PATTERNS
- For this a rake is essential. (Sometimes a bucket and spade set comes with a plastic rake.)
- With your spade or a stick, draw a large pattern, clearly divided into sections.
- 'Colour in' the darker sections by raking them.
- View your art from a sand dune or cliff if you can.

## SAND SCULPTING
- This involves building up shapes to make a raised sculpture (a sandcastle is the classic sand sculpture).
- Pile up damp sand using a spade then shape it with your hands and pat it down smoothly.
- Go for simple, rounded shapes or animals such as turtles, whales or dolphins.
- Add detail using collected items such as shells, pebbles, seaweed, driftwood or feathers.

## SAND SILHOUETTES
- This needs a bucket or bag of very dry sand collected from the top of the beach.
- Place an object (or person) down flat on damp sand and pour the dry sand all around its edges.
- Take away the object or person and, hey presto, you have a mysterious silhouette!

# Driftwood sculptures

You can only really do this if you find yourselves on a wild beach where lots of driftwood and interesting objects have been washed up on the shore.

## Stuff you need

- **A beach with lots of large pieces of driftwood**
- **Flotsam and jetsam**
- **A camera or phone**

## Tips

- Avoid rusty metal or sharp objects
- Keep away from hazardous waste and patches of tar
- Leave your sculpture to inspire others (or let the sea eat it!)

## Get started

**1. Explore the beach first and see what you can find. The kinds of washed-up materials you can use to make a big beach sculpture are:**

- Large pieces of driftwood
- Clean fishing nets
- Clean crates
- Old bits of rope
- Seaweed
- Sticks

2. Collect as much of this together as you can then start to move it around, finding ways to build it up from the ground and fix it together so that it stands up and looks dramatic.

**3. Use bits of rope, netting or even seaweed to lash poles together, or tie crates to your structure.**

4. You do not have to make an animal or recognisable object – some of the best driftwood sculptures are big, wacky abstract designs.

# Beach games

Here are loads of different games to play on the sand – what's your favourite?

## PEBBLE RINGS

With a stick or spade, draw six circles in the sand and mark a number in each. Mark a line a few metres away. Grab six small pebbles each and try to land one in each circle. Who can get the most?

## BEACHY NOUGHTS AND CROSSES

Mark a 3x3 grid in the sand with a spade or stick then play the classic game, drawing in the sand.

## PEBBLE GOLF

Dig nine small holes each about 10 metres apart in a really big circle. Mark each one with a stick or other object. Find a small pebble each and aim for the first hole. Count how many 'shots' it takes you to get around the course – the lowest total wins.

## FRISBEE SKITTLES

You need a Frisbee and something to use as skittles: plastic bottles, sticks, cricket stumps or flip-flops stuck in the sand. Mark a line, take turns and see who can knock over the skittles.

## OTHER GAMES

Try cricket, rounders, catch, volleyball, keepy-uppy, tennis, long jump, triple jump, French cricket or boules (ask an adult if you don't know the rules).

## SPLASH RELAY

Get into two teams. Each team needs a bucket and a cup (they need to be the same size). In relay fashion, players run to the sea, scoop up a cup of water and dash back. The first team to fill the bucket wins.

# GAMES TO PLAY

Outdoor games are the best because there's more space to run around and have fun. Enjoy trying out these cracking outdoor games.

# Limbo

Limbo is a dance contest that started on the Caribbean island of Trinidad. The idea is to pass under a bar, facing forwards, without touching the floor with your hands. Whoever gets under the lowest bar (without knocking it off or falling over) wins. The world record is 21.59 cm!

## Stuff you need

• 3 long garden canes (2m long)
• Some clothes pegs
• A marker pen or pencil

## Get started

1. This needs to be done on grass. Push two of the canes into the grass about 1.5m apart for the uprights.

2. Ask the tallest person to stand next to one of the canes and make a mark on it at her or his chin height. Label this 1.

3. You now need to make numbered marks down this cane, equally spaced. A good way to do this is to use the width of a shoe. Put the shoe across the cane just under the 1 mark and make a new mark (2) under the shoe. Do this all the way down the cane then repeat on the other upright cane.

4. Fix the pegs at mark 1 then rest the bar (the third cane) on them. You are ready to limbo!

5. Start at 1 and let everyone go under the bar in turn, forwards. Then move the bar down to mark 2 and so on. Whoever goes the lowest is the winner.

# Footbag

Footbag is a really simple and fun game because you can play it on your own or with a small group. You will need to buy or make a footbag, though!

## Get started

1. Here's a simple way to make a footbag with old tights.

2. First cut one leg off the tights with the scissors, so you have a long sock.

3. Pour a small cupful of dried lentils into the long sock and shake them to the bottom of the foot.

4. Hold the tights just above the lentils then spin the bottom (the ball of lentils) around several times so there is a good twist in the tights.

5. Keeping a hold of both parts, push the ball of lentils back up into the leg part of the tights, pushing it right through so the whole thing is inside out.

## Stuff you need

- A pair of old nylon tights (ask before you cut them up!)
- A small cupful of lentils or other dry beans
- Scissors

6. Repeat this several times: twisting and pushing the ball of lentils back through so you build up lots of layers of nylon around the lentils.

7. When there's about 10-15cm of loose tights left, twist this and tie a couple of very tight knots. Pull them hard and cut off any loose end. You now have a footbag!

## To play

Footbag is like keepy-uppy with a football. You have to gently kick and flick the bag to keep it in the air. You can use any part of your foot or your knee or leg. Hands or arms are not allowed! Can you keep it in the air? Can you pass between friends? Look at some footbag videos online to see how it's done.

# Obstacle course

Making your own obstacle course is even better than trying one at a park or playground – here's how.

## Get started

**1** An obstacle course is best done on grass. First lay out as many things as you have room for. What to choose (and the order) is really up to you.

**2** Ideas to include:

⊙ Something to jump over (e.g. a cane resting on two chairs, a large empty box, a towel laid longways or, if you are big, a small paddling pool with water!)

### Stuff you need

Lots of things are listed below but none of them are essential

⊙ Something to crawl through (e.g. some garden netting tied down at the edges, a play tunnel, a big box with the ends opened out or a sheet weighed down at the sides)

⊙ Something to squeeze under (e.g. a garden chair, a bench, string tied between trees)

⊙ Something to step between (e.g. a ladder laid flat, a line of hoops or tyres, a few mats spaced out)

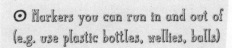

⊙ Markers you can run in and out of (e.g. use plastic bottles, wellies, balls)

⊙ Something to balance along (eg a rope laid on the grass, a thick beam of wood fixed by an adult, a plank).

• Other ideas:
⊙ Toss a ball or rolled up sock into a bucket
⊙ Dodge a swinging water-filled balloon hanging from a tree
⊙ Incorporate a climbing frame, trampoline or slide into your obstacle course
⊙ Use a paddling pool as a water obstacle

**3** Try out the course and if you like you can time each other through it, using a stopwatch (mobile phones have these). Award home-made medals or small prizes if you wish.

# Capture the boot

This is a top game to play outside at any time of year, providing you have enough space. It's best played with at least four people. A large back garden or park with trees is the perfect place.

## Get started

1 Someone is chosen to be the guard. This person must guard the boot, which is placed somewhere near the middle of the garden or space.

2 The idea is that the other players spread out and hide (while the guard counts to 50 with their eyes closed), then try and sneak up and capture the boot without being seen.

3 The guard can move around and if he or she spots a person, can run back to the boot and call out the person's name. A player who is caught this way is out unless he or she can reach the boot before the guard.

114

4 The winner is the first one to grab the boot or the last one who is out. The winner takes over as the guard (or you can simply take turns so everyone has a go).

# Torch tag

This game can also be played in the dark if everyone has a torch (it's sometimes called torch tag). Everyone must keep their torch on but the guard must correctly identify a person to get him or her out.

# Sponge bombs

This is something to do in the garden on a hot day. Be warned, you are going to get very, very wet!

## Get started

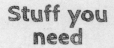
**1** It's really best to wear a swimming costume (or old clothes at least) to play this.

**2** Each person will need a bucket or plastic bowl half-filled with water (warm or cold).

**3** Each person will need two or three sponges (you can cut big ones in half, but ask first).

**4** Each person goes to a corner of the garden, the oldest shouts 'go' and you throw the sponges, trying to soak each other. It's as simple as that.

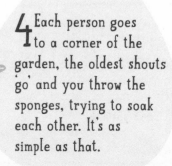

# Splat catch

Splat catch is a fantastic game to play outdoors in the summer. Be warned — it's another one where you might get wet...

## Stuff you need

• 2-3 packets of water balloons (water bombs)
• A bucket

## Get started

1. This is a good game to play at a party where there are at least 10 people. You can play it with just two but it's much more fun with a crowd.

2. You'll need a big garden or a safe open space like a park or playing field.

3. Ask an adult or two to help you fill and tie all of the water bombs. Put them all in a bucket.

4. Each person needs a partner to play and everyone must stand opposite their partner, about 2 metres apart in two lines. Each pair needs one water bomb.

5. Have a little practice at throwing and catching with your partner.

6. To start the game properly, the water bombs must start all on the same side. The person on the far left must throw the balloon to his or her partner to catch. This carries on down the line one at a time, so everyone can see.

7. Anyone whose balloon bursts is out. If you drop it or miss a catch but it doesn't burst, you are still in.

8. After the last person has been, both lines take a large step back. This time the throws go the other way, starting from the end that finished last.

9. When everyone has been, take another step back. Keep doing this until there is only one pair left — the winners!

# A4 race

This is a race with a difference and it's a bit potty too. It's also one where children might be able to beat adults!

## Stuff you need

- Pieces of A4 paper (used or new, any colour)
- String

## Get started

**1** There is only one rule with the A4 race: you can only move on paper. Anyone who touches the ground is out.

**2** First mark the start and finish with two lines of string laid on the ground. You can use something else if you don't have any string handy. The course can be short or long.

**3** One person is chosen to be the race judge.

**4** The racers line up at the start – each person must have two pieces of A4 paper.

**5** Players race by putting one piece of paper down on the ground and stepping on it then placing the second one in front and stepping onto that (then picking up the first piece again and so on). Sliding the paper along with your feet is not allowed.

**6** First one to reach the finish wins, but the judge decides if anyone is out.

# Snake in the loo

This is a sitting down game to play around a camp fire, or on the beach or in the car when you're on your way to an outdoor adventure.

## Get started

1. Any number can play and you don't need anything to set it up.

2. A funny situation is chosen and everyone takes turns to think of funny responses or solutions.

3. For example:

Player 1: Situation: you find a snake in the loo.

Player 2: Flush and keep flushing.

Player 3: Arrrrghhh!

Player 4: Wait till it's finished.

Player 1: Next time, take a crocodile with you.

Player 2: Tell your sister the toilet is free.

Player 3: Ask it to clean the washbasin as well.

Player 4: Ask Dad if your next house can be not in the jungle.

4. The turns continue until someone is stuck. There are no winners or losers in the game.

## Situations to use

It's fun to make up your own but here are some ideas to get you started:

- **There are three people but only one Rolo left**
- There are ants in your pants
- **The Queen comes round for tea**
- Granny becomes a biker
- **The shops run out of chocolate**
- You fall in the lake on a school trip
- **Someone gives you 500 coconuts**
- There's an alien under your bed
- **It rains mince**

# Sock golf

Sock golf is MUCH easier than real golf – you don't need golf clubs, a ball, a golf course or even those funny trousers.

## Stuff you need

- **A sock for each person, rolled into a ball**
- A variety of large containers such as: bins, buckets, a wheelbarrow, a big plastic bowl, large cardboard boxes, trays with sides and baskets (nine in total)
- **A pen or pencil each**
- A scorecard each
- **Paper and sticky tape**

## Get started

1 Spread the containers around the garden, spaced as far apart as you can.

2 Each one needs to be numbered, from 1 to 9. Do this by writing numbers on pieces of paper and taping them to the containers.

3 Decide on a starting point, about 5-10 metres from container 1.

4 The idea is to throw your rolled sock into the containers in the smallest number of throws. You always take the next throw from where the previous throw landed, like golf.

**5** Each player must write down his or her score for each 'hole' (container) – which is the number of throws taken to land in it. You'll need to make some cards like the one below.

**6** After hole 9, add up your score – the person with the lowest total score wins. It's fun to try and beat your own record too.

**7** You can also play this with small soft toys instead of socks: teddy golf!

| HOLE | SCORE |
|------|-------|
| 1 | |
| 2 | |
| 3 | |
| 4 | |
| 5 | |
| 6 | |
| 7 | |
| 8 | |
| 9 | |
| TOTAL | |

# Blind man's splash

This is a game to play outside on a nice hot day, in swimming costumes because you are going to get VERY wet. It's for four people and it's monster fun!

## Stuff you need

- Two water pistols or squirty water bottles
- Two blindfolds
- Two buckets of water

## Get started

1 Choose two teams of two.

2 Put down the buckets of water a few metres apart.

3 Blindfold one person from each pair. The other person in the pair helps their partner.

4 Call 'go', spin the two blindfolded players around and give them an empty water pistol each.

5 The idea is that each 'guide' shouts to his or her partner where to go, first to fill up the water pistol and then where to aim to soak the other blindfolded player.

6 The first one to hit the other wins the game. Swap over and enjoy the shootout!

# Soaky-soaky

This is another game where everyone ends up soaking wet as the name suggests. Play it outside on a sunny day with swimming togs – you need at least three people but the more the merrier.

## Stuff you need

- A bucket of water
- A plastic beaker
- Paper and pen
- A hat
- Towels

## Get started

1 Write the numbers 1 to 10 on small pieces of paper and put these in the hat.

2 Choose someone to be the first Soaker. He or she takes a number from the hat, in secret, then puts it back.

3 The Soaker fills the beaker with water and then all the other players stand in a circle around him or her, about five paces away.

4 The players take it in turn to say any number between 1 and 10. Numbers can't be repeated.

5 The Soaker splashes whoever says the secret number. That person then becomes the Soaker and takes a new secret number from the hat.

123

# Paper chase

If you are having an outdoor party with lots of people this game works well. A big garden with plenty of bushes, trees, hedges etc. works best.

## Stuff you need

- 10-20 sheets of paper, any type
- Scissors
- Polythene bags or carrier bags (one per player)
- A pen
- Some small prizes

## Get started

**1** This is a game that needs to be set up in advance by an adult, so be nice to one and give them these instructions in good time!

**2** The paper needs to be cut into strips 2-3cm wide then each strip cut into pieces about 8cm long although these dimensions don't matter at all.

**3** Write PRIZE on 3-4 pieces (depending on how many prizes you have), or draw a special symbol that you've decided means 'PRIZE'. Or it's fun to have 3-4 prize pieces which are a different colour – like golden tickets.

**4** An hour or two before the game, the adult in charge needs to sneak out and distribute the paper pieces all over the garden or park, hiding them in bushes, under hedges, behind gnomes and so on. Keep one to show everyone playing at the start.

**5** When ready, give everyone a polythene bag, show them the paper strip and set them off to find as many as they can. The winner is the person who collects the most (plus anyone who finds a prize ticket).

**6** Younger children can be paired with older partners.

# Talk

Let everyone have a say:

Have you ever had any outdoor game calamities?

What kind of games are your worst nightmare and why?

What's your favourite outdoor game?

If you could be champ at any outdoor game what would you pick?

# Choose

Which would you rather play?

Twister or giant dominoes?

Hide and seek or tree climbing?

Croquet or badminton?

Rounders or bug safari?

Treasure hunt or water pistol shootout?

Skittles or a penalty shoot-out competition?

# Score

Rate these A, B, C, D, E or Z:

Giant Jenga

Sand pit

Tree house

Rope swing

Paddling pool

Football goal

Tipi

Basketball hoop

Climbing frame

# Jokes

Lots of kids love playing hide and seek.
What do these love playing?

| | |
|---|---|
| Mice | Hide and squeak |
| Spies | Hide and sneak |
| Skunks | Hide and reek |
| Scaredy-cats | Hide and shriek |
| Old boats | Hide and leak |
| Haunted castle doors | Hide and creak |
| Computer boffins | Hide and geek |
| Fashion designers | Hide and chic |
| Naked runners | Hide and streak |

# Fun facts

Six things you should know about flying discs (Frisbees):

**1** Plastic flying discs were first sold by Walter Frederick Morrison who got the idea after someone saw American students throwing metal pie tins to each other.

**2** Some early Frisbees were sold as 'Pluto Platters' and were made to look like UFOs.

**3** Frisbees are named after Frisbie pies, which came in tins that flew well.

**4** Disc-catching competitions for dogs are popular in the USA. One of the biggest is the Skyhoundz DiscDogathon Championships.

**5** Sports played with flying discs include: Disc golf, Dodge disc, Flutterguts, Fricket, Hot box and Schtick.

**6** The world record distance for a flying disc throw is 338 metres. That's a LONG way.

# WINTER FUN

Most of us spend a lot of time indoors in winter and outside it can be dark, cold, wet and dreary. BUT... there are still loads of marvellous outdoor things you can do in winter. Some are magical and unmissable, so read the list and get prepared to have some serious fun.

## Go on a mud walk

Most of the time we avoid mud but if you are dressed for it and prepared to get mucky then you can really enjoy the brown, squelchy stuff.

### Get started

1. The first thing is to decide where to go. Many popular footpaths are muddy in winter so look for places where lots of people like to walk:
- Through woods
- In parks
- Countryside paths
- Places near rivers, streams, ponds or lakes
- Footpaths which cross farms which keep animals

### Stuff you need
- Old clothes or outdoor gear/waterproofs that can easily be washed
- Hats and gloves
- Wellies (essential!)
- A walking stick each (make one if you haven't got one)

2. Decide on a route. 1.5-5 kilometres (about 1-3 miles) is a good length of walk – stepping through mud is slower than ordinary walking so take that into account!

3. Use your walking stick to test the depth of mud, puddles, boggy areas and slimy grass. If you go deeper than your wellies then you'll be very cold, wet and miserable!

4. Use your walking stick to help you balance – mud can be very slippery!

5. Try to clean the mud off your wellies before you step back inside at the end: wipe them on long grass, slosh them in a puddle or use a garden hose to wash the soles.

# Go sledging

What could be more fun than whizzing down a dazzling white hill at speed with your friends?

## Stuff you need

- A snowy hill
- A sledge
- Warm clothes including a hat and gloves (wellies are best too)

## Get started

1. The first thing is to find a good sledging spot – pick a slope that is:
   - Not too steep
   - Without a road or wall/fence/water at the bottom
   - Not too crowded
   - Not covered in trees or bushes.

2. Make sure that you know how to steer a sledge. To go left, press your left foot into the snow and to go right press down with your right foot!

3. Have a little practice on a quiet, gentle slope if you've not been sledging before. Sit in the sledge rather than lying down. Always make sure you have a clear run when you sledge – make sure there's no chance of you bumping into someone or something.

4. Plastic sledges work quite well on soft, powdery snow. Traditional wooden sledges with metal runners are good on packed down, harder snow – they do go very fast. Sliding down a hill on a big plastic sheet is a giggle but it cannot be steered!

# Make a snowbeast

Making a snowman is one of the great pleasures of winter but next time it snows, what about making a snowbeast? Here are some ideas for creating a creature extraordinaire!

## Get started

1. First, decide what kind of beast you want to make. Here are some ideas:
• A real animal, such as a bear, cat, rabbit, pig, penguin, hedgehog or dog
• A monster or made-up creature
• An alien or robot.

2. The best way to build the body is by rolling a big snowball. Press together a few big handfuls of snow into a rough ball shape then roll this in the snow, changing direction to make it round and strong.

3. You can either use the trowel to carve the snowball into your beast shape or build up the creature by adding smaller snowballs and packing handfuls of snow where needed.

4. Use sticks or vegetables to add details like eyes, noses and antennae.

## Stuff you need

• Plenty of snow
• A garden trowel
• Warm clothes including a hat, gloves and wellies
• Twigs and small dark stones

## Tips

• Plump, round creatures work best – don't try and make a snow giraffe!
• Pat the snow down gently at each stage to make it stronger.
• Make sure you take photos!

131

# Snow lantern magic

Snow lanterns aren't easy to make but they look really magical outside on a crisp, snowy evening. You will need adult help with this project, though.

## Get started

1. There are two ways to make snow lanterns. The first way is the easiest: you roll a large snowball until it's about the size of a football. Leave it on the ground and hollow out a space in its top using the spoon. The space you hollow out should be as large as a grapefruit.

 2. Ask an adult to put a tea light (a small, sturdy candle) into the space and light it when it's dark outside.

Your lantern should glow nicely! Make a line of snow lanterns for a lovely effect.

3. The second way to make snow lanterns is harder and slower but looks great. You start by making about 20 snowballs (the size of a small apple). Arrange seven

## Stuff you need

- **Plenty of snow**
- Tea lights (plus matches and tapers)
- **Metal table spoons**
- Warm clothes including a hat, gloves and wellies

of them in a circle so they have a small gap between them. Place an unlit tea light in the centre.

4. Add a second layer of small snowballs, placing them across the gap so they make a smaller circle, leaning in a little (we are aiming for a kind of pyramid shape). Do the same again, adding more until the top of the pile is closed.

5. Ask an adult to light the tea light with a taper when it's getting dark outside.

 Again, a line of these lanterns makes a special sight.

# Ice pendants

This is a craft activity that you can try if the weather is below freezing, so check the weather forecast before you attempt it!

## Get started

1 Put all of the containers on the tray and take them outside. Pour water into them so that there is 2-3 cm of water in each container.

2 Drop your decorations into the water: berries, small leaves etc.

3 Cut one piece of string for each container, about 30-40cm long. Place these so that each container has one end of a piece of string dangling in the water.

4 Place the tray on the ground outside away from the house where the water can freeze. Leave it overnight and if the temperature drops below zero then you should have some ice pendants!

5 Carefully remove the pendants from the containers and hang them outside from a tree or washing line.

## Stuff you need

- Different shallow containers such as plastic cups, lids, small bowls or dishes
- A jug or bottle of water
- Natural items for decoration such as berries, small flowers, petals, leaves, grass, tiny stones
- String and scissors
- A tray

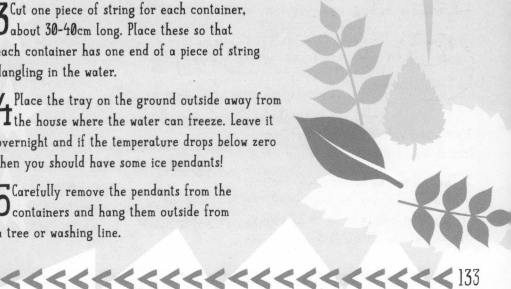

# Talk

Chat about these and compare your answers.

☛ What's your favourite thing about winter?

☛ What's your least favourite thing about winter?

☛ Would you like to visit the Arctic or Antarctic one day?

☛ Are you a penguin or a polar bear person?

# Choose

Jumping in snow or sliding on ice?

Skating or sledging?

Snowballing or making a snowman?

Skiing or snowboarding?

Snowmobile or dog sled?

Cold drinks or hot drinks?

# Make a snow maze

If just a small amount of snow falls it's no good for building snowmen or igloos but it is good for creating a mysterious snow maze. Here's how to do it.

## Stuff you need

- **A light falling of snow**
- Warm clothes including a hat, gloves and wellies

## Get started

1. Mazes are puzzles where you have to find your way to the end (sometimes that's in the middle). For some designs for mazes see the Beach mazes on page 104.

2. A snow maze needs to be quite simple – something like this:

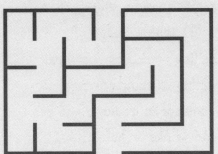

3. The maze is best done on grass. Mark out your lines by walking along them leaving a clear trail of footprints in the snow.

4. To make the lines clearer you can roll a snowball along the lines so the snow is picked up. 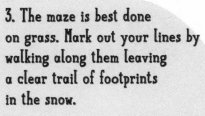 When it gets too big, throw it away and start a new one. Then try out your maze!

# Catch leaves

## Stuff you need
- Some tall trees

You might be surprised, but this is actually excellent fun and also a tricky challenge. It's really an autumn activity rather than winter but let's not worry about that!

## Get started

**1** Leaf-catching is best done in autumn, and the ideal kind of day is one with a gentle breeze. It's almost impossible to do this on a really windy day, and leaves fall less often on windless days.

**2** A park is the perfect place for leaf-catching. You need tall trees away from roads and traffic. The trees should have already started to shed their leaves.

**3** Once you've got all this in place then you can do leaf-catching. The challenge is simple: can you catch a falling leaf before it hits the ground? Sounds simple? No way! Leaves don't fall straight – they flutter and loop around making it really hard. But don't give up.

**4** If you are good and succeed then try a different kind of tree. See if you can catch a range of leaves. If you can then you are THE CHAMPION.

# Other winter outdoor activities to try

### 1. SNOW PAINTING
Fill a hand-held sprayer with water and add some food colouring. Spray the snow and create a winter picture or pattern.

### 2. SNOWBALL SKITTLES
Set up a line of empty plastic bottles or cans from the recycling box and see how long it takes you to knock them all over with snowballs.

### 3. TRACK WILDLIFE
Snowy ground is a great place to find and follow animal tracks. You can track rabbits or deer or all sorts of creatures (see the chart on page 56 to identify animal footprints).

### 4. JUMP IN A SNOWDRIFT
If it has been windy as well as snowy you may be able to find snowdrifts. These are deep banks of snow blown by the wind. You can find them in exposed places next to walls or on the side of hills. Test the depth with a stick and jump in!

### 5. MAKE SNOW ANGELS
Lie on your back in deep snow with your arms and legs spread out. Move your arms and legs from side to side and you should leave a wonderful snow angel print. Just make sure you're in waterproofs and wrapped up toasty warm!

## Love, hate or meh?

Muddy winter walks    Early nights    Wellies    Hail

Frost    Wrapping up in scarf,    The north wind    Snow

Log fires    hat and gloves    Christmas shopping

# Ice Facts

1. You can make clear ice by freezing boiled bottled water.

2. Queen Victoria sometimes used ice imported by ship from the USA.

3. Ice is less dense than water. If it was heavier then ice in frozen lakes and rivers would sink and this could continue until it killed all of the living things in the water.

4. Antarctica is covered by a monster sheet of ice that is over 3.2 kilometres (2 miles) thick in places.

5. The world's biggest iceberg was larger than Cyprus.

# Jokes

**What's an ig?**
A snow house
without a loo

**What do Mexican
snowmen eat?**
BRRR-itos

**What's the fastest
type of pullover?**
A ski jumper

**What do
snowmen eat?**
Icebergers

**What's a Roman's
favourite weather?**
Hail Caesar

# Fun list

If it snows you can throw snowballs. What can you throw if...

| | |
|---|---|
| You're in a bakery? | **Doughballs** |
| **You've got extra feet?** | Toeballs |
| You're in a boat? | **Rowballs** |
| **You're a rook?** | Crowballs |
| You're Robin Hood | **Bowballs** |
| You're not fast? | Slowballs |
| **You're Santa?** | **Ho-ho-ho-balls** |

# ACTIVITY CHALLENGES

Are you ready for a challenge? This section contains bigger and longer outdoor family activities to try: expeditions, tasks, walks, rides, things to learn and to have a go at. Some of these might take a half day or even a whole day and will need to be planned in advance.

The challenges are arranged in THREE levels: Easy, Harder and Tough. You can tick them off when you have done them – just make sure there's an adult with you all the time!

# Level 1 Challenges (Easy)

## ☐ 1. Build a bivouac

A bivouac is a small temporary shelter, which you build and then take down when you have finished with it. It's a good challenge to build a bivouac in the woods. You can even sleep in it!

### Stuff you need
- Strong string or rope
- Two waterproof sheets
- Some rocks or heavy branches

### What to do

- Find two sturdy trees close together.
- Tie a rope between them about 1 metre off the ground.
- Drape a sheet over this in a tent shape and weigh it down with stones or logs.
- Put the other sheet inside the shelter and spend some time in your bivouac!

## ☐ 2. Roll down a grass hill

Rolling down a hill is a great giggle, but only if you choose the right hill!

### Stuff you need
- Clothes that can take a few grass stains or muddy patches

### What to do

- Only attempt this in nice dry, warm weather!
- You need a hill covered in soft, springy grass. A country park is a good place to look.
- Make sure it has no sharp stones, thorny branches, holes, puddles, cowpats or dog muck.
- If it's OK then roll away!

## ☐ 3. Fly a kite

Kites are simple, cheap, clever, colourful and excellent to fly. You can even have a go at making your own.

### Stuff you need
• A kite and an adult to help you

### What to do
• It's very important that you only fly kites well away from overhead power lines (poles, pylons, cables, sub-stations and so on).
• Pick an open site such as a beach or playing field or large country park.
• If it's a new kite, read the instructions carefully. They'll tell you how to get launched.
• Let the line out and start flying your kite!

## ☐ 4. The Matchbox 20 Challenge

This is a fantastic little task that you can do outdoors in all sorts of places.

### Stuff you need
• An empty matchbox for each person

### What to do
• The challenge is very simple: to collect 20 tiny items and fit all of them inside a matchbox.
• All the objects must be different.
• They must all be collected outside.
• Ask someone to check your matchbox when you have finished.

## ☐ 5. Clean a local park

Here's a challenge that is not just for you but it's something that will help other people as well.

### Stuff you need
- Suitable outdoor clothes
- Gloves and strong bin bags
- You might also want to buy some cheap litter pickers too
- A camera or phone for taking 'before and after' photos

### What to do
- This is a good activity to do with a family or a larger group, so you can really make a difference.
- Each person will need a bag.
- Pick up paper, crisp bags, plastic wrappers, cans and small bits of litter. Leave large items to the adults and avoid glass items, rusty or sharp metal or anything heavy.
- Take the bags to a recycling centre and recycle what you can. Don't fill up the park rubbish bins!

## ☐ 6. Grow potatoes

Potatoes are really easy to grow and they taste fantastic – much better than ones from the shops. This activity needs to be done in the spring.

### Stuff you need
- Seed potatoes to plant (from a garden centre – choose 'early' ones)
- A patch of soil OR you can grow them in a large container or a plastic sack (you'll need to buy compost if you don't have soil)

### What to do
- You'll see little shoots or 'eyes' on the seed potatoes. Plant them when these are about 2cm long.
- In the soil, dig holes 10-15cm deep and put one potato in each hole. Or you can dig a trench. The potatoes should be about 30cm apart.
- Get your container, fill it ¾ full with soil or compost (or a mix) and plant the potatoes 15cm apart, 15cm deep. Make sure there are drainage holes in the bottom of the bag or container.
- Water the potatoes when the soil is dry. Your yummy crop should be ready to dig up in mid summer or when the leaves start to fade. This should take between 10 and 20 weeks from when you plant.

## 7. Do a 2-kilometre walk

If you treat your walk like an expedition, with things to spot or games to play along the way, you'll enjoy it all the more!

### What to do

• **Ask a grown up to help you plan your 2-kilometre walk. You can search online for local walks or choose your own route.**

• A nice idea is to aim for a place about a kilometre away and then walk there and back.

• **Take this book then if there's not much to see, you can do some of the talk/choose/score activities or word games along the way.**

### Stuff you need

• **A map if you don't know the area well**
• Suitable shoes (not flip flops)
• **Suitable clothes for the weather**
• A drink if it's hot

### Stuff you need

• Stones – they should be bigger than 50p coins but smaller than your hand

## 8. Balance five stones

This is a tricky challenge. For a start you need to find somewhere where there are lots of stones!

### What to do

• This is another of those challenges which is simple to try but not easy to achieve. The best place to do it is a rocky beach. You might also find stones by small streams and in hilly places.

• You just need to balance five stones in a little tower, one on top of the other.

• **Choose your stones with care! Round ones are going to be horrible to balance... lumpy ones difficult.**

• No sneaky cheats by finding five pieces of flat slate either – that's banned!

## ☐ 9. Follow an ancient road or track

There are very old tracks all over the place which have been walked for thousands of years. The hardest part is finding them to start with.

### What to do

• Your local library is a good place to start: look in the 'Local history' section for books that include old maps or paths.
• You can also look online. In a search engine type 'Roman roads' followed by the place where you live.
• Try and find an old track or path which is away from traffic. Walk along it and look out for any clues that the path has been there for a long time.

### Stuff you need
• A detailed map of the area you are in, such as an Ordnance Survey map (libraries have these)

### Stuff you need
• Nettles (a small bagful of leaves)
• An onion
• A veg stock cube
• Milk
• A hob, saucepan, wooden spoon and blender

## ☐ 10. Make and eat nettle soup

Yes, nettles are rotters when they sting you – but they are also edible and make quite a tasty soup. At least they are cheap!

### What to do

• Nettle soup is best made in spring with young nettle plants. Don't use tall old ones or pick the leaves later than June.
• Wear gloves, long sleeves and long trousers for picking nettles. Pick the top 4-6 leaves off each stem and wash them well.
• With help from an adult, in a pan, gently fry the chopped onion in some butter then add a pint of boiling water. Crumble in the stock cube and simmer for 10 mins.
• With gloves, add the nettle leaves plus a cup of milk, bring to the boil and stir. After 5 mins, blend the soup, add salt and pepper and enjoy!

## ☐ 11. Do a 5-kilometre bike ride

If you find a nice, quiet route away from traffic and go with someone who knows the way, a bike ride can become a fun little adventure.

### Stuff you need

- A helmet
- A bike
- A drink

### What to do

- Ask an adult you know to help you plan a good safe route. A map is a great help here.
- See if you can find a cycle track off-road, or a bridleway — search online for these.
- Make sure your bike is ready for the trip (check the brakes and tyres!).
- Travel in a group and ride in single file. Make sure you don't leave anyone behind.

## ☐ 12. Plant a tree

Planting a tree and seeing it grow over the years is a wonderful thing to do. Trees not only give us clean air but they gobble up carbon dioxide too!

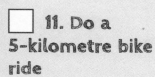

### Stuff you need

- A sapling (young tree)
- A spade or trowel
- A watering can

### What to do

- First you need to find a good place to plant a tree. If there's space in your garden, plant it well away from buildings. If you want to plant it in the countryside, contact the Woodland Trust who will help you.
- One way to grow a tree is to collect seeds in autumn, such as conkers or acorns, then plant these in pots. In spring you can plant out any young trees that sprout.
- You can also go to a garden centre and buy a young tree such as an apple tree. Ask for advice and follow the instructions with the tree.
- It's best not to plant trees in summer — they like lots of water. Spring or autumn is best.

# Level 2 Challenges (Harder)

## ☐ 1. Build a den

You can, of course, make a den by throwing some blankets over some furniture but the most satisfying dens are the ones you build from natural materials that you collect.

### What to do

- There are some plans for building dens in the Garden Fun section of the book. You can try the 'bird hide' method on page 10.
- One way to start is to make a wigwam of three or four long sticks or branches, tying them with string at the top.
- Wrap string around the structure (leaving an entrance) and hang leafy branches from the strings to make walls.
- Put a waterproof sheet inside and you have a den!

### Stuff you need

- Branches
- Sticks
- String
- Scissors
- A waterproof sheet

## ☐ 2. Five at keepy-uppy

### Stuff you need

- A football
- Plenty of room outside

Juggling a football looks easy when some people do it – but can you keep a ball in the air for five kicks?

### What to do

- A good practice for keepy-uppy is to drop a ball onto your foot to kick up and catch.
- Try doing this with both feet – the secret is not to bend your knee but to flick your foot up with a fairly straight leg.
- Keep trying until you get a feel for the ball (it can take a while).
- Have a go at five kicks, using the same foot flick and both feet.

### ☐ 3. Climb a tree

Climbing a tree is one of the things in life that everyone who is able to should do. You might even meet a friendly squirrel up there.

**Stuff you need**
- Grippy shoes
- A welcoming tree

### What to do

- This is all about picking the right tree. Choose a tree that:
  - ✚ Has plenty of low branches
  - ✚ Is not too small and bendy
  - ✚ Has soft grass under it, in case you tumble.
- Avoid climbing a tree when it's wet, windy or dark!
- Stay low while you get used to it and make sure someone is with you in case you get stuck.

### ☐ 4. Explore a cave

Caves are mysterious, exciting and often amazing, especially ones that go deep underground. Here's how to get started.

**Stuff you need**
- A cave
- Possibly a torch

### What to do

- Finding a good cave is the hardest part. There are caves along cliffs in the coast but these are usually too dangerous to visit. The best caves are those where you get taken round by a guide.

## ☐ 5. Go on a night walk through the woods

There is something truly memorable about creeping through a forest in the dark. Just don't go alone!

### Stuff you need
- Good shoes or wellies for walking (woods are often muddy)
- A coat
- A good torch

### What to do
- Offer to do the washing up then ask a friendly parent/carer if they will take you on a little adventure into some woods at night.
- Go to some local woods you know, where there's a footpath, or use a map to plan a short route.
- Spring or autumn are probably the best times to go, when it's dark fairly early but not too cold.
- Watch out for owls, foxes, badgers and deer – it helps if you're not noisy!

## ☐ 6. Clean a beach

This is another 'community' challenge that helps keep our environment looking good and shows kindness to others.

### Stuff you need
- Wellies if it's winter, warm outdoor clothes, gloves and strong bin bags
- Litter pickers (these are great and can be bought cheaply from discount hardware stores)

### What to do
- To really make a difference, do this activity with the whole family or even a larger group.
- Each person will need a bag.
- Pick up paper, wrappers, cans, plastic bottles and small bits of litter. Leave large items to the adults and avoid anything sharp or heavy.
- Take the bags to a recycling centre and recycle what you can. Don't fill up nearby rubbish bins!

## ☐ 7. Walk across a moor

Moors are wild and woolly (and beautiful) places.
But if you go to one, be prepared for some
wild and woolly weather!

### What to do

• Do a bit of research to find out where the
nearest moorland is to you.
• Use a map to plan a route, but check the weather
forecast as well. Remember that most moors are very
hilly so don't try and go too far!

### Stuff you need
• Warm clothing
• Walking boots
or wellies
(moors are
often boggy)
• A hat

## ☐ 8. Find some wild clay and make a pot

Wild or natural clay is clay that you dig up out of the ground
yourself. Be prepared to get very dirty, so wear old clothes.

### Stuff you need
• A bucket
• A spade
• A trowel
• Smooth wooden
boards

### What to do

• To find wild clay you need to dig in an area of clay soil.
Search online for a map of clay soils.
• Clay is usually covered with other kinds of soil so the best
place to find it is the banks of small shallow stream or ditches.
• If the clay is dry, leave it in water for a while. Remove any
stones or bits of leaves and twigs then work it with your hands,
rolling it into a ball the size of an apple.
• To make a pot, push your thumb into the ball then
squeeze between your fingers and thumb to make the
hole bigger, turning the pot as you go.

## ☐ 9. Kayak around a lake

Paddling in a canoe on open water is very exciting and here's how to do it safely.

### Stuff you need
- A buoyancy aid (life jacket)
- Warm clothing
- A kayak!

### What to do
- You can hire kayaks and life jackets at lots of lakes where boats are allowed.
- This activity should only be done under the close supervision of a kayak instructor or an adult who has lots of experience. Avoid windy days and cold weather (summer is the best time).
- If you have never done it before then stay close to your instructor and stay near to the shore.
- Listen for instructions and take your time.

## ☐ 10. Sleep on a beach

Here's a family activity which is different, exciting, adventurous, wild, intriguing, fun, challenging and, well, you'll only find out what else if you try it!

### Stuff you need
- A bivvy bag (an outdoor sleeping bag) each
- A pillow and warm clothing

### What to do
- The first thing is to find a quiet beach where you are allowed to sleep. A parent/carer will need to check local bye-laws or ask permission if the beach is private.
- You can only sleep on a beach which has plenty of dry sand well away from the sea. Don't pick a beach with cliffs or walls or rocks.
- This is best done in the summer on a quiet night. Check the weather forecast and stay at home if it's going to be wet, windy or there's going to be a high tide!
- You'll need to set up your camp at the top of the beach, well above the high water mark or you'll get very wet! Remember to wrap up warm as it can get cold outside at night even in summer.

## 11. Catch a crab

Fancy a nippy little challenge? Crabbing will keep you busy for ages, especially if you have a competition to find the biggest crab.

### What to do
- The best places to catch crabs are on piers or sea walls, or deep rock pools.
- Tie your bait carefully to one end of the string and lower it into the water so it rests on the bottom.
- Wait a few minutes then slowly pull up your string. Try and net your crab before it drops off the line!
- Put it in a bucket of seawater so you can get a close look, then return it to the sea afterwards.

### Stuff you need
- String
- Some bait (bits of bacon or ham are good)
- A bucket
- A fishing net

## 12. Forage for a meal

Finding wild food is very satisfying if you know where to look (and know how to identify things). Here are some ideas to get started.

### What to do
- For beginners, the best time to forage is the autumn when there's plenty of wild fruit around.
- Here are some plants which are easy to identify:

  Blackberries
  Bilberries (also called blaeberries, whinberries or whortleberries)
  Damsons
  Hazelnuts
  Sweet chestnuts
  Crab apples

### Stuff you need
- Plastic containers (with lids) or carrier bags

- If you're not sure what they look like, go with someone who knows. You can also use a guidebook or look up pictures of them online.
- Some of the foods need to be cooked – look in library books or online for recipes. Always wash foods before eating them and don't eat anything you can't identify for certain.

## Stuff you need

• A tent and all the usual camping equipment!

## 13. Camp in a forest

Camping in a forest is an exciting thing to do, especially if you are in a quiet place well away from other people.

## What to do

• Ask an adult to check the rules for wild camping in your area. In some places wild camping is allowed, whereas in others you will need to ask permission of the landowner, or use an established campsite.

• Don't pitch your tent on uncomfortable tree roots!

• Make sure you ask if you are allowed to have a camp fire.

## 14. Cook on a camp fire

Nothing tastes as good as food cooked on an open fire. Just make sure you have permission to light a fire first and that an adult is in charge of the fire.

## What to do

• You need to raise the metal grill above the fire so either make the fire in a hole or balance the grill on bricks, green logs or large stones.

• Let the fire die down a bit – don't try to cook on leaping flames or everything will be burnt.

• The easiest way to cook is to use pans on top of the grill: try baked beans, pasta (serve with ketchup and grated cheese) or a stew started off at home (serve with crusty bread). Potato curry is yummy too!

• You can also cook things wrapped in foil: veg kebabs, corn on the cob with butter, fish.

• Grill sausages or toast teacakes or marshmallows using forks tied to sticks with wire (these will get very hot – be careful!).

## Stuff you need

• A BBQ grill (or metal oven shelf)
• Pans
• Utensils
• Foil
• Food
• Water
• Bowls and cutlery
• Wood
• Matches

## 15. Do a 8-kilometre walk

Ah, eight kilometres doesn't sound much does it? If you can walk eight kilometres, you'll not only have done well, you'll probably have seen lots of interesting things along the way.

### What to do

• Ask an adult to help plan your walk. You can search online for local walks or choose your own route (8km is 5 miles).
• A circular walk means that you get to see more. Try and include hills so you get some views.
• **Take this book along so you can try do some of the word games and talking activities along the way.**
• If you manage all 8 kilometres, request a chocolate reward: you've earned it!

### Stuff you need
• Good shoes for walking (strong trainers or walking boots – not wellies)
• Waterproofs
• **A backpack**
• A map
• A snack
• A drink

### Stuff you need
• **A helmet**
• Bike
• **Clothes suited to the weather**
• A drink

## 16. Do a 10-kilometre bike ride

Try and find a cycle track away from roads and you'll really enjoy exploring on your bike.

### What to do

• Ask an adult to help you plan a good route avoiding traffic.
• See if you can find a cycle track off-road, or a bridleway – search online for these or use an Ordnance Survey map.
• **Make sure your bike is ready for the trip (check tyre pressure and brakes).**
• Travel in a group and ride in single file. Make sure you don't leave anyone behind.

# Level 3 Challenges (Tough!)

## ☐ 1. Sleep under the stars

Sleeping outdoors without a tent gives you a chance to see the night sky like you've never seen it before (if it's not cloudy that is).

### What to do

• This is definitely a summer activity (although it can be quite cold on summer nights outdoors too). And it's an activity that must be done with an adult.

• You can, of course, sleep outside in the garden but often there's too much light pollution to see the stars well. It's much better if you can do this out in the countryside.

• **Look at the weather forecast and choose a night with clear skies if possible and no chance of rain. You also need to find a location where you're allowed to sleep overnight (sometimes called wild camping).**

• It's very important to make sure that you are warm enough!

### Stuff you need
• A bivvy bag (waterproof sleeping bag)
• Foam mat
• **Pillow**
• Warm clothes

## ☐ 2. Dam a stream

This is another classic old-school outdoor challenge which depends on finding the right place. Be prepared to get rather wet...

### Stuff you need
• Wellies
• Towels
• **A change of clothes**

### What to do

• The best streams to try and dam are in hilly areas out in the countryside. You need a small, shallow stream where the water is just a few centimetres deep and not flowing too fast. There need to be lots of stones around.

• Beware sharp or slimy stones.

• Make a line of rocks across the stream and keep adding them until you have slowed down the flow (look out – this makes the water deeper!).

• At the end take your dam apart to protect the river banks and wildlife.

## ☐ 4. Ride a horse

Horses are amazing creatures and to have a go at riding will give you a memorable experience. It takes a little time but you will get a real sense of achievement if you do it. Have a go!

## What to do

• **The best way to start is to find a riding school near you. You can search online for this, perhaps asking an adult to help you.**
• In the UK, if you go to a British Horse Society riding school then you'll be in safe hands. They ensure that the horses are well looked after and the instructors are qualified.
• **At the riding stables ask about beginning lessons: what is involved, what it costs and what you need to do it.**
• Meet some friendly horses and have a go.

### Stuff you need
• A horse! (see below for where to find one)

## ☐ 3. Row across a lake

If you've never rowed a boat before then you'll probably do lots of laughing and going round in circles to start with. It's all part of the fun...

## What to do

• **This is another activity best done in warm weather.**
• Make sure you have an adult with you who can keep you safe and give you help if needed.
• **Lots of lakes have boats for hire.**
• You go backwards when rowing so make sure the person with you keeps their eyes out for other vessels!

### Stuff you need
• A small rowing boat
• A buoyancy aid (life jacket)
• Warm clothing

# ACTIVITY CHALLENGES

## ☐ 5. Climb a 1000-ft hill

Climbing a hill of over 1000 feet (305 metres) is a real achievement and you'll also get the reward of great views from the top.

### What to do

• The first thing is to find a hill over 1000ft high!
• Plan your walk: use a map, stick to footpaths and take it slowly. Have rests on the way up and enjoy conquering your peak!

### Stuff you need

• Good shoes or boots for walking (with a grippy sole)
• Warm clothes
• Waterproofs
• A drink and a snack

## ☐ 6. Camp out in the wilderness

Camping in the garden or on a campsite is fun but camping out in the wild is special!

### What to do

• The first thing to do is some research: find out where you can go wild camping in the countryside. One way to do this is to search online for 'wild camping'.
• Once you have found a suitable place out in the wild away from other people, check the weather forecast and take everything you need. Enjoy the peace and adventure!

### Stuff you need

• A tent
• Sleeping bags
• Warm clothes and all the usual camping gear

## ☐ 7. Catch a fish with a net

Fish are not easy to catch, which is why this challenge is in the tough category. Do you have the patience, cunning and skill to do it?

### Stuff you need
• A fishing net
• Some bait (such as small pieces of bread)

### What to do
• Find a suitable pond, river or lake and make sure you have permission from whoever owns the land.
• It's best to go with an adult who knows something about fishing!
• **Stand somewhere safe and keep quiet and still.**
• If you catch a fish in your net, remember to put it back quite quickly as fish can only live a very short time out of water.

## ☐ 8. Do a 12-kilometre walk

A 12-kilometre walk will take you several hours, but it will also provide you with a chance to explore somewhere you can't reach by car or bike.

### Stuff you need
• Good shoes for walking (strong trainers or walking boots)
• Waterproofs
• **A backpack**
• A map
• A snack and a drink

### What to do
• **Ask an adult to help plan your walk.** With the right map you can plan a route along footpaths, or you can search the web for walks in the countryside.
• Remember that in winter and spring, paths are often very muddy. It's a good idea to take a walking stick if there is likely to be mud (it can stop you slipping over).
• **If you manage to finish the walk, give yourself a nice treat at the end!**

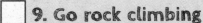

### ☐ 9. Go rock climbing

Indoor climbing walls are good fun but there is nothing like grappling your way up a real rock face outside in the hills. Here's how to do it safely.

## Stuff you need

- **Loose warm clothes**
- Trainers with good grip

## What to do

- **Ask an adult to help you find out where you go to try rock climbing supervised by trained instructors. Lots of places have special kids' climbing sessions.**
- Helmets, ropes and safety equipment are provided so that there's no danger of a fall even if you slip. Can you conquer the final challenge?

# ANSWERS

## Challenge

(p54)

These are some of the words you can make with the letters of WILDLIFE:

Fed, lid, few, ill, lie, dew, elf, led, wed, die

Dell, file, idle, life, wide, will, fill, wife, dill, fled, lied, wild, fell, flew, well

Dwell, filed, field, filled, willed.

# FURTHER INFORMATION

## Books to read

These books have more outdoor activities, facts and fun:

*100 Family Adventures* by Tim Meek and Kerry Meek (Frances Lincoln 2015)

*101 Things For Kids To Do Outside* by Dawn Isaac (Kyle Books 2014)

*The Wild City Book: Fun Things To Do Outdoors In Towns And Cities* by Jo Schofield and Fiona Danks (Frances Lincoln 2014)

*RSPB Wildlife In Your Garden* by Mike Dilger (Bloomsbury 2016)

*The Usborne Outdoor Book* by Alice James and Emily Bone (Usborne 2016)

## Websites

Where to find out more interesting stuff to do outdoors:

**50 Things to do before you're 11¾** www.50things.org.uk – a great site to set you off on your outdoor escapades. Can you tick off all 50?

Do Try This at Home http://www.dotrythisathome.com/ – one family goes on lots of adventures, and shares their ideas

**Fossil Hunting in the UK** www.ukfossils.co.uk – discover hundreds of places to look for fossils, plus lots of advice about how to find them and about fossil-hunting events

Wild camping in Scotland www.visitscotland.com/see-do/activities/walking/wild-camping – all the info you need to find a wild campsite

12/8/17 CAERLEON

# ALSO AVAILABLE BY ANDY SEED:

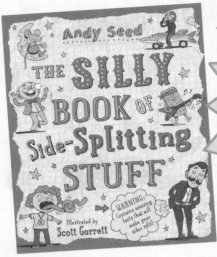

**WARNING:**
**CONTAINS AMAZING FACTS THAT WILL MAKE YOUR SIDES SPLIT!**
This laugh-out-loud book is bursting with silly lists, facts, jokes and funny true stories all about animals, inventions, food and much more. Find out about The Great Stink, the man who ate a bike, the world's richest cat and a sofa that can do 101mph. Unmissable!

**WINNER OF THE BLUE PETER BOOK AWARDS**

£5.99 ISBN 978-1-4088-5079-4

**WARNING:**
**THESE BOOKS WILL CURE ALL BOREDOM!**
Andy Seed's laugh-out-loud 'Anti-Boredom' series has something for everyone. A seemingly endless car journey? A boring rainy afternoon? A dull holiday? Or even a boring time in the run-up to Christmas? Andy's got an activity, a joke or a game for that! These witty and wacky books are bursting with funny facts, games, quizzes and things to do for hours of fun.

£5.99 ISBN 978-1-4088-5076-3
978-1-4088-7010-5

160